W9-BNG-216

BOOK SOLD
NO LONGER R.H.P.L.
PROPERTY

RICHMOND HILL
PUBLIC LIBRARY

DEC 29 2015

CENTRAL LIBRARY
905-884-9288

CAPITALISM

CAPITALISM

Edited by Richard Smalbach

Britannica®
Educational Publishing

IN ASSOCIATION WITH

ROSEN
EDUCATIONAL SERVICES

Published in 2015 by Britannica Educational Publishing (a trademark of Encyclopædia Britannica, Inc.) in association with The Rosen Publishing Group, Inc.
29 East 21st Street, New York, NY 10010

Copyright © 2015 by Encyclopædia Britannica, Inc. Britannica, Encyclopædia Britannica, and the Thistle logo are registered trademarks of Encyclopædia Britannica, Inc. All rights reserved.

Rosen Publishing materials copyright © 2015 The Rosen Publishing Group, Inc. All rights reserved.

Distributed exclusively by Rosen Publishing.
To see additional Britannica Educational Publishing titles, go to rosenpublishing.com.

First Edition

Britannica Educational Publishing
J.E. Luebering: Director, Core Reference Group
Anthony L. Green: Editor, Compton's by Britannica

Rosen Publishing
Hope Lourie Killcoyne: Executive Editor
Richard Smalbach: Editor
Nelson Sá: Art Director
Nicole Russo: Designer
Cindy Reiman: Photography Manager
Amy Feinberg: Photo Researcher
Introduction and supplementary material by Richard Barrington.

Library of Congress Cataloging-in-Publication Data

Capitalism/edited by Richard Smalbach.
       pages cm. — (Political and economic systems)
Includes bibliographical references and index.
ISBN 978-1-62275-359-8 (library bound)
1. Capitalism—Juvenile literature. I. Smalbach, Richard.
HB501.C24225415 2015
330.12'2—dc23
                                                                2014010598

Manufactured in the United States of America

On the cover, p. 3: *Picsfive/Shutterstock.com*

are permitted—even encouraged—to improve their material condition. Individuals cannot have such aims, much less such "rights," until the dominant authority of custom or hierarchical privilege has been swept away. A rearrangement of this magnitude entails wrenching dislocations of power and prerogative. A market society is not, consequently, merely a society coordinated by markets. It is, of necessity, a social order with a distinctive structure of laws and privileges.

It follows that a market society requires an organizing principle that, by definition, can no longer be the respect accorded to tradition or the obedience owed to a political elite. This principle becomes the generalized search for material gain—a striving for betterment that is unique to each individual. Such a condition of universal upward striving is unimaginable in a traditional society and could be seen only as a dangerous threat in a society built on established hierarchies of authority. But, for reasons that will be seen, it is accommodated by, and indeed constitutive of, the workings of a market system.

The process by which these institutional and attitudinal changes are brought about constitutes a grand theme—perhaps the grand theme—of economic history from roughly the 5th to the 18th and even into the 19th century in Europe. In terms of political history, the period was marked by the collapse of the Roman Empire, the rise of feudalsim, and the slow formation of national states. In social terms, it featured the end of an order characterized by an imperial retinue at the top and massive slavery at the bottom, that order's replacement by gradations of feudal vassalage descending from lord to serf, and the eventual appearance of a bourgeois society with distinct classes of workers, landlords, and entrepreneurs. From the economist's perspective, the period was marked by the breakdown of a coordinative mechanism of centralized

Feudalism preceded capitalism. This system of rights and obligations was characterized by the bond between lords and vassals and was based on land ownership. With the formation of nation states, feudalism gave way to a society with distinct classes of workers, landlords, and entrepreneurs. Universal Images Group/Getty Images command, the rise of the mixed pressures of tradition and local command characteristic of the feudal manor, and the gradual displacement of those pressures by the material penalties and rewards of an all-embracing market network. In this vast transformation the rise of the market mechanism became crucial as the means by which the new social formation of capitalism ensured its self-provisioning, but the mechanism itself rested on deeper-lying social, cultural, and political changes that created the capitalist order it served.

To attempt to trace these lineages of capitalism would take one far beyond the confines of the present subject. Suffice it to remark that the emergence of the new order was first given expression in the 10th and 11th centuries, when a rising mercantile "estate" began to bargain successfully for recognition and protection with the local lords and monarchs of the early Middle Ages. Not until the 16th and 17th centuries was there a "commercialization" of the aristocratic strata, many of whose members fared poorly in an ever more money-oriented world and accordingly contracted marriages with wealthy merchant families (whom they would not have received at home a generation or two earlier) to preserve their social and material status. Of greatest significance, however, was the transformation of the lower orders, a process that began in Elizabethan England but did not take place en masse until the 18th and even the 19th century. As feudal lords became profit-minded landlords, peasants moved off the land to become an agricultural proletariat in search of the best wages obtainable because traditional subsistence was no longer available. Thus, the market network extended its disciplinary power over "free" labour—the resource that had previously eluded its influence. The resulting social order made it possible for markets to coordinate production and distribution in a manner never before possible.

The Evolution of Capitalism

Greater individual freedoms and the existence of profit incentives were key conditions that allowed a capitalist system to take root. From there, the development of a fully capitalist system was a gradual process, and one that continues to this day. The following sections detail some of the major stages in that process.

From Mercantilism to Commercial Capitalism

It is usual to describe the earliest stages of capitalism as mercantilism, the word denoting the central importance of the merchant overseas traders who rose to prominence in 17th- and 18th-century England, Germany, and the Low Countries. In numerous pamphlets, these merchants defended the principle that their trading activities buttressed the interest of the sovereign power, even when, to the consternation of the court, this required sending "treasure" (bullion) abroad. As the pamphleteers explained, treasure used in this way became itself a commodity in foreign trade, in which, as the 17th-century merchant Thomas Mun wrote, "we must ever observe this rule; to sell more to strangers than we consume of theirs in value."

For all its trading mentality, mercantilism was only partially a market-coordinated system. Adam Smith complained bitterly about the government monopolies that granted exclusive trading rights to groups such as the East India or the Turkey companies, and modern commentators have emphasized the degree to which mercantilist economies relied on regulated, not free, prices and wages. The economic society that Smith described in *The Wealth of Nations* in 1776 is much closer to modern society, although it differs in many respects, as shall be seen. This 18th-century stage is called "commercial capitalism," although it should be noted that the word *capitalism* itself does not actually appear in the pages of Smith's book.

Smith's society is nonetheless recognizable as capitalist precisely because of the prominence of those elements that had been absent in its mercantilist form. For example, with few exceptions, the production and distribution of all goods and services were entrusted to market forces rather than to the rules and regulations that had abounded a century earlier. The level of wages was likewise mainly determined by the interplay of the supply of, and the demand for, labour—not by the rulings of local magistrates. A company's earnings were exposed to competition rather than protected by government monopoly.

Adam Smith. Scottish National Portrait Gallery, Edinburgh, Scotland/The Bridgeman Art Library

Perhaps of greater importance in perceiving Smith's world as capitalist as well as market-oriented is its clear division of society into an economic realm and a political realm. The role of government had been gradually narrowed until Smith could describe its duties as consisting of only three functions: (1) the provision of national defense, (2) the protection of each member of society from the injustice or oppression of any other, and (3) the erection and maintenance of those public works and public institutions (including education) that would not repay the expense of any private enterpriser, although they might "do much more than repay it" to society as a whole. And if the role of government in daily life had been delimited, that of commerce had been expanded. The accumulation of capital had come to be recognized as the driving engine of the system. The expansion of "capitals"— Smith's term for firms—was the determining power by which the market system was launched on its historic course.

Thus, *The Wealth of Nations* offered the first precise description of both the dynamics and the coordinative processes of capitalism. The latter were entrusted to the market mechanism—which is to say, to the universal drive for material betterment, curbed and contained by the necessary condition of competition. Smith's great perception was that the combination of this drive and counterforce would direct productive activity toward those goods and services for which the public had the means and desire to pay while forcing producers to satisfy those wants at prices that yielded no more than normal profits. Later economists would devote a great deal of attention to the question of whether competition in fact adequately constrains the workings of the acquisitive drive and whether a market system might not display cycles and crises unmentioned in "The Wealth of Nations." These were questions unknown to Smith because the institutions that would produce them, above all the development of large-scale industry, lay in the future. Given these historical realities, one can only admire Smith's perception of the market as a means of solving the economic problem.

Smith also saw that the competitive search for capital accumulation would impart a distinctive tendency to a society that harnessed its motive force. He pointed out that the most obvious way for a manufacturer to gain wealth was to expand his enterprise by hiring additional workers. As firms

expanded their individual operations, manufacturers found that they could subdivide complex tasks into simpler ones and could then speed along these simpler tasks by providing their operatives with machinery. Thus, the expansion of firms made possible an ever-finer division of labour, and the finer division of labour, in turn, improved profits by lowering the costs of production and thereby encouraging the further enlargement of the firms. In this way, the incentives of the market system gave rise to the augmentation of the wealth of the nation itself, endowing market society with its all-important historical momentum and at the same time making room for the upward striving of its members.

One final attribute of the emerging system must be noted. This is the tearing apart of the formerly seamless tapestry of social coordination. Under capitalism two realms of authority existed where there had formerly been only one— a realm of political governance for such purposes as war or law and order and a realm of economic governance over the processes of production and distribution. Each realm was largely shielded from the reach of the other. The capitalists who dominated the market system were not automatically entitled to governing power, and the members of government were not entrusted with decisions as to what goods should be produced or how social rewards should be distributed. This new dual structure brought with it two consequences of immense importance. The first was a limitation of political power that proved of very great importance in establishing democratic forms of government. The second, closer to the present theme, was the need for a new kind of analysis intended to clarify the workings of this new semi-independent realm within the larger social order. As a result, the emergence of capitalism gave rise to the discipline of economics.

Adam Smith

After two centuries, Adam Smith remains a towering figure in the history of economic thought. Known primarily for a single work—*An Inquiry into the Nature and Causes of the Wealth of Nations* (1776), the first comprehensive analysis of political economy—Smith is more properly regarded as a social philosopher whose economic writings constitute only the capstone to an overarching view of political and social evolution.

Much more is known about Adam Smith's thought than about his life. He was born in 1723, the son by second marriage of Adam Smith, comptroller of customs at Kirkcaldy, Scotland, a small (population 1,500) but thriving fishing village near Edinburgh, and Margaret Douglas, daughter of a substantial landowner.

At the age of 14, in 1737, Smith entered the University of Glasgow, already remarkable as a centre of what was to become known as the Scottish Enlightenment. Graduating in 1740, Smith won a scholarship (the Snell Exhibition) and traveled on horseback to Oxford, where he stayed at Balliol College. His years there were spent largely in self-education, from which Smith obtained a firm grasp of both classical and contemporary philosophy.

Returning to his home after an absence of six years, Smith cast about for suitable employment. The connections of his mother's family, together with the support of the jurist and philosopher Lord Henry Kames, resulted in an opportunity to give a series of public lectures in Edinburgh—a form of education then much in vogue in the prevailing spirit of "improvement." The lectures, which ranged over a wide variety of subjects from rhetoric to history and economics, made a deep impression on some of Smith's notable contemporaries. They also had a marked influence on Smith's own career, for in 1751, at the age of 27, he was appointed professor of logic at Glasgow, from which post he transferred in 1752 to the more remunerative professorship of moral philosophy, a subject that embraced the related fields of natural theology, ethics, jurisprudence, and political economy.

Smith then entered upon a period of extraordinary creativity, combined with a social and intellectual life that he afterward described as "by far the happiest, and most honourable period of my life." During the week he lectured daily from 7:30 to 8:30 AM and again thrice weekly from 11 AM to noon, to classes of up to 90 students, aged 14 to 16. Afternoons were occupied with university affairs in which Smith played an active role, being elected dean of faculty in 1758; his evenings were spent in the stimulating company of Glasgow society.

In 1759 Smith published his first work, *The Theory of Moral Sentiments*. Didactic, exhortative, and analytic by turns, it lays the psychological foundation on which *The Wealth of Nations* was later to be built. In it Smith described the principles of "human nature," which, like other leading philosophers of his time, he took as a universal and unchanging datum from which social institutions, as well as social behaviour, could be deduced.

In Glasgow, Smith's friends included several prominent inventors, businessmen, and philosophers, and he later expanded this circle of influences in his travels on the European continent. In 1776, Smith published his most famous work, *The Wealth of Nations*. *The Wealth of Nations* was received with admiration by Smith's wide range of friends and colleagues, although it was by no means an immediate popular success. The work finished, Smith went into semiretirement, living a quiet life until he died in 1790.

Over the years, Smith's lustre as a social philosopher has escaped much of the weathering that has affected the reputations of other first-rate political economists. Although he was writing for his generation, the breadth of his knowledge, the cutting edge of his generalizations, and the boldness of his vision have never ceased to attract the admiration of all social scientists, economists in particular. Couched in the

(continued on the next page)

spacious, cadenced prose of his period, rich in imagery and crowded with life, *The Wealth of Nations* projects a sanguine but never sentimental image of society. Smith is the very epitome of the Enlightenment: hopeful but realistic, speculative but practical, always respectful of the classical past but ultimately dedicated to the great discovery of his age—progress.

From Commercial to Industrial Capitalism

Commercial capitalism proved to be only transitional. The succeeding form would be distinguished by the pervasive mechanization and industrialization of its productive processes, changes that introduced new dynamic tendencies into the economic system while significantly transforming the social and physical landscape.

The transformative agency was already present in Smith's day, observable in a few coal mines where steam-driven engines invented by Thomas Newcomen pumped water out of the pits. The diffusion and penetration of such machinery-driven processes of production during the first quarter of the 19th century has been traditionally called "the" Industrial Revolution, although historians today stress the long germination of the revolution and the many phases through which it passed. There is no doubt, however, that a remarkable confluence of advances in agriculture, cotton spinning and weaving, iron manufacture, and machine-tool design and the harnessing of mechanical power began to alter the character of capitalism profoundly in the last years of the 18th century and the first decades of the 19th.

The alterations did not affect the driving motive of the system or its reliance on market forces as its coordinative principles. Their effect was rather on the cultural complexion

William Blake referred to industrial factories as "dark Satanic mills." Library of Congress, Washington, D.C.

of the society that contained these new technologies and on the economic outcome of the processes of competition and capital accumulation. This aspect of industrialization was most immediately apparent in the advent of the factory as the archetypal locus of production. In Smith's time the individual enterprise was still small—the opening pages of *The Wealth of Nations* describe the effects of the division of labour in a 10-man pin factory—but by the early 19th century the increasing mechanization of labour, coupled with the application of waterpower and steam power, had raised the size of the workforce in an ordinary textile mill to several hundreds; by mid-century in the steel mills it was up to several thousands, and by the end of the century in the railways it was in the tens of thousands.

The increase in the scale of employment brought a marked change in the character of work itself. In Smith's day the social distance between employer and labourer was still sufficiently small that the very word *manufacturer* implied an occupation (a mechanic) as well as an ownership position. However, early in the 19th century William Blake referred to factories as "dark Satanic mills" in his epic poem *Jerusalem*, and by the 1830s a great gulf had opened between the manufacturers, who were now a propertied business class, and the men, women, and children who tended machinery and laboured in factories for 10- and 12-hour stints. It was from the spectacle of mill labour, described in unsparing detail by the inspectors authorized by the first Factory Act of 1802, that Marx drew much of the indignation that animated his analysis of capitalism. More important, it was from this same factory setting, and from the urban squalor that industrialization also brought, that capitalism derived much of the social consciousness—sometimes revolutionary, sometimes reformist—that was to play so large a part in its subsequent political life. Works such as Charles Dickens's "Hard Times" (1854) depicted the factory system's inhumanity and the underlying economic doctrines that supposedly justified it. While these works brought attention to the social problems stemming from industrialization, they also tended to discount the significant improvements in the overall standard of living (as measured by the increases in life expectancy and material comforts) that accompanied modernization. Country life of just a generation earlier had been no less cruel, and in some respects it was more inhuman than the factory system being criticized. Those critics who failed to compare the era of industrialization with the one that immediately preceded it also failed to account for the social and economic progress that had touched the lives of ordinary people.

The degradation of the physical and social landscape was the aspect of industrialization that first attracted attention, but it was its slower-acting impact on economic growth that was ultimately to be judged its most significant effect. A single statistic may dramatize this process. Between 1788 and 1839 the output of pig iron in Britain rose from 68,000 to 1,347,000 tons. To fully grasp the significance of this 20-fold increase, one has to consider the proliferation of iron pumps, iron machine tools, iron pipes, iron rails, and iron beams that it made possible; these iron implements, in turn, contributed to faster and more dependable production systems. This was the means by which the first Industrial Revolution promoted economic growth, not immediately but with gathering momentum. Thirty years later this effect would be repeated with even more spectacular results when the Bessemer converter ushered in the age of steel rails, ships, machines, girders, wires, pipes, and containers.

The most important consequence of the industrialization of capitalism was therefore its powerful effect on enhancing what Marx called "the forces of production"—the source of what is now called the standard of living. The Swiss economic demographer Paul Bairoch calculated that gross national product (GNP) per capita in the developed countries rose from $180 in the 1750s (in dollars of 1960 purchasing power) to $780 in the 1930s and then to $3,000 in the 1980s, whereas the per capita income of the less-developed countries remained unchanged at about $180–$190 from 1750 to 1930 and thereafter rose only to $410 in 1980. (This seemingly persistent gap between the richest and the poorest countries, which contradicts the predictions of the standard theory of economic growth, has increasingly occupied the attention of contemporary economists. Although the question is answered in part by explaining that the rich countries have experienced industrialization and the poor ones have not, the question remains why some have experienced industrialization and others have not.)

The development of industrialization was accompanied by periodic instability in the 18th and 19th centuries. Not surprisingly, then, one side effect of industrialization was the effort to minimize or prevent economic shocks by linking firms together into cartels or trusts or simply into giant integrated enterprises. Although these efforts dampened the repercussions of individual miscalculations, they were insufficient to guard against the effects of speculative panics or commercial convulsions. By the end of the 19th century, economic depressions had become a worrisome and recurrent problem, and the Great Depression of the 1930s rocked the entire capitalist world. During that debacle, GNP in the

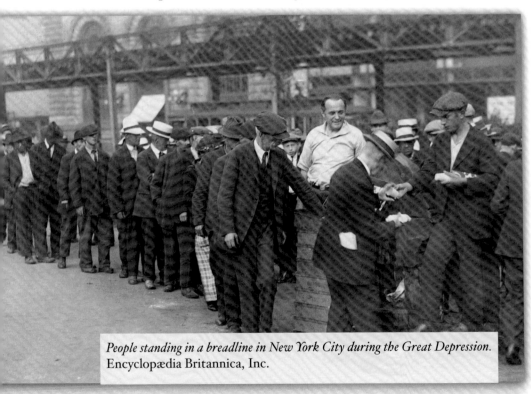

People standing in a breadline in New York City during the Great Depression. Encyclopædia Britannica, Inc.

United States fell by almost 50 percent, business investment fell by 94 percent, and unemployment rose from 3.2 to nearly 25 percent of the civilian labour force. Economists have long debated the causes of the extraordinary increase in economic instability from 1830 to 1930. Some point to the impact of growth in the scale of production evidenced by the shift from small pin factories to giant enterprises. Others emphasize the role of miscalculations and mismatches in production. And still other explanations range from the inherent instability of capitalist production (particularly for large-scale enterprises) to the failure of government policy (especially with regard to the monetary system).

From Industrial to State Capitalism

The perceived problem of inherent instability takes on further importance insofar as it is a principal cause of the next structural phase of the system. The new phase is often described as state capitalism because its outstanding feature is the enlargement in size and functions of the public realm. In 1929, for example, total U.S. government expenditures—federal, state, and local—came to less than one-tenth of GNP; from the 1970s they amounted to roughly one-third. This increase is observable in all major capitalist nations, many of which have reached considerably higher ratios of government disbursements to GNP than the United States.

At the same time, the function of government changed as decisively as its size. Already by the last quarter of the 19th century, the emergence of great industrial trusts had provoked legislation in the United States (although not in Europe) to curb the monopolistic tendencies of industrialization. Apart from these antitrust laws and the regulation of a few industries of special public concern, however, the functions of the federal government were not significantly broadened from Smith's vision. Prior to the Great Depression, for example, the great bulk of federal outlays went for defense and international relations, for general administrative expense and interest on the debt, and for the post office.

The Great Depression radically altered this limited view of government in the United States, as it had earlier begun to widen it in Europe. The provision of old-age pensions, relief for the hungry and poor, and a dole for the unemployed were all policies inaugurated by the administration of President Franklin D. Roosevelt, following the example of similar enlargements of government functions in Britain, France, and Germany. From the 1970s onward, such new kinds of federal spending—under the designation of Social Security, health, education, and welfare programs—grew to be 20 to 50 percent larger than the traditional categories of federal spending.

Thus, one very important element in the advent of a new stage of capitalism was the emergence of a large public sector expected to serve as a guarantor of public economic well-being, a function that would never have occurred to Smith. A second and equally important departure was the new assumption that governments themselves were responsible for the general course of economic conditions. This was a change of policy orientation that also emerged from the challenge of the Great Depression. Once regarded as a matter beyond remedy, the general level of national income came to be seen by the end of the 1930s as the responsibility of government, although the measures taken to improve conditions were on the whole timid, often wrongheaded (such as highly protectionist trade policies), and only modestly successful. Nonetheless, the appearance in that decade of a new economic accountability for government constitutes in itself sufficient reason to describe capitalism today in terms that distinguish it from its industrial, but largely unguided, past.

There is little doubt that capitalism will continue to undergo still further structural alterations. Technological advances are rapidly reducing to near insignificance the once-formidable barriers and opportunities of economic geography. Among the startling consequences of this technological leveling of the world have been the large displacements of high-tech manufacturing from Europe and North America to the low-wage regions of Southwest Asia, Latin America, and Africa. Another change has been the unprecedented growth of international finance to the point that, by the beginning of the 21st century, the total value of transactions in foreign exchange was estimated to be at least 20 times that of all foreign movements of goods and services. This boundary-blind internationalization of finance, combined with the boundary-defying ability of large corporations to locate their operations in low-wage countries, poses a challenge to the traditional economic sovereignty of nations, a challenge arising from the new capabilities of capital itself.

A third change again involves the international economy, this time through the creation of new institutions for the management of international economic trade. A number of capitalist nations have met the challenges of the fast-growing international economy by joining the energies of the private sector (including organized labour) to the financial and negotiating powers of the state. This "corporatist" approach, most clearly evident in the organization of the Japanese economy, was viewed with great promise in the 1980s but in the 1990s was found to be severely vulnerable to opportunistic behaviour by individuals in both the public and the private sectors. Thus, at the onset of the 21st century, the consensus on the economic role of government in capitalism shifted back from the social democratic interventionism of the Keynesian system and the managed market economies of the "Asian tigers" (countries such as Hong Kong, Singapore, Malaysia, and South Korea that experienced rapid growth in the late 20th century) to the more noninterventionist model of Adam Smith and the classical economists.

It is not necessary, however, to venture risky predictions concerning economic policy. Rather, it seems more useful to posit two generalizations. The first emphasizes that capitalism in all its variations continues to be distinguished from other economic systems by the priority accorded to the drive for wealth and the centrality of the competitive mechanism that channels this drive toward those ends that the market rewards. The spirit of enterprise, fueled by the acquisitive culture of the market, is the source of the dynamism of capitalism. The second generalization is that this driving force and constraining mechanism appear to be compatible with a wide variety of institutional settings, including substantial variations in the relationships between the private and public sectors. The form of capitalism taken also differs between nations because the practice of it is embedded within cultures; even the forces of globalization and the threat of homogenization have proved to be more myth than reality. Markets cater to national culture as much as national culture mutates to conform to the discipline of profit and loss. It is to this very adaptability that capitalism appears to owe its continued vitality.

The Great Depression's Economic Impact

The most devastating impact of the Great Depression was human suffering. In a short period of time, world output and standards of living dropped precipitously. As much as one-fourth of the labour force in industrialized countries was unable to find work in the early 1930s. While conditions began to improve by the mid-1930s, total recovery was not accomplished until the end of the decade.

The Great Depression and the policy response also changed the world economy in crucial ways. Most obviously, it hastened, if not caused, the end of the international gold standard. Although a system of fixed currency exchange rates was reinstated after World War II under the Bretton Woods system, the economies of the world never embraced that system with the conviction and fervour they had brought to the gold standard. By 1973, fixed exchange rates had been abandoned in favour of floating rates.

Both labour unions and the welfare state expanded substantially during the 1930s. In the United States, union membership more than doubled between 1930 and 1940. This trend was stimulated by both the severe unemployment of the 1930s and the passage of the National Labour Relations (Wagner) Act (1935), which encouraged collective bargaining. The United States also established unemployment compensation and old-age and survivors' insurance through the Social Security Act (1935), which was passed in response to the hardships of the 1930s. It is uncertain whether these changes would have eventually occurred in the United States without the Great Depression. Many European countries had experienced significant increases in union membership and had established government pensions before the 1930s. Both of these trends, however, accelerated in Europe during the Great Depression.

In many countries, government regulation of the economy, especially of financial markets, increased substantially in the 1930s. The United States, for example, established the Securities and Exchange Commission (1934) to regulate new stock issues and stock market trading practices. The Banking Act of 1933 (also known as the Glass-Steagall Act) established deposit insurance in the United States and prohibited banks from underwriting or dealing in securities. Deposit insurance,

(continued on the next page)

which did not become common worldwide until after World War II, effectively eliminated banking panics as an exacerbating factor in recessions in the United States after 1933.

The Great Depression also played a crucial role in the development of macroeconomic policies intended to temper economic downturns and upturns. The central role of reduced spending and monetary contraction in the Depression led British economist John Maynard Keynes to develop the ideas in his *General Theory of Employment, Interest, and Money* (1936). Keynes's theory suggested that increases in government spending, tax cuts, and monetary expansion could be used to counteract depressions. This insight, combined with a growing consensus that government should try to stabilize employment, has led to much more activist policy since the 1930s. Legislatures and central banks throughout the world now routinely attempt to prevent or moderate recessions. Whether such a change would have occurred without the Depression is again a largely unanswerable question. What is clear is that this change has made it unlikely that a decline in spending will ever be allowed to multiply and spread throughout the world as it did during the Great Depression of the 1930s.

Modern Disruptive Forces

The evolution of capitalist systems has been shaped from time to time by disruptive forces. Although the word sounds destructive, in an economic context, a disruption simply means anything that powerfully shakes up the existing order of things. In terms of the history of the development of capitalism, the achievement of individual freedom and the Industrial Revolution can be seen as disruptive forces. More recently, two more modern disruptive forces have guided the continuing development of capitalism: the information age, and globalization.

These disruptive forces are linked by more than just chronology. To a large extent, information technology helped facilitate globalization by making communication and the transfer of capital between nations virtually instantaneous. In turn, information technology also helped to offset some of the negative impacts of globalization, by creating new, information-based industries to help replace jobs in traditional sectors, such as manufacturing, that were increasingly being transferred from rich-world nations to poorer nations.

The following is a look at the disruptive roles of information technology and globalization in more detail.

Information Technology

The advent of innovative computer and communications technology toward the end of the 20th century ushered in a new era dominated by information rather than industry. Just as land, labour, and machinery had been the capital of an industrial age, information became a new form of capital in modern business.

During the 1970s and 1980s, a number of new telecommunications advances came into existence, including modern communications satellites. Telephone companies, cable television stations, and other media outlets began using these satellites to transmit data around the world. By the late 1990s, integrated digital networks were being developed to create a global voice, data, text, and video system. At the same time, large computer networks, such as the Internet, permitted modems—devices that transmit data through phone lines—to link individual computers to other computers throughout the world. In 1993, Internet usage exploded when commercial providers were first allowed to sell Internet connections to individuals.

Information technology has radically changed capitalism in two ways. Some of the world's most successful companies, such as Apple, Google, Facebook, and Amazon, are firms that led the way in providing entirely new products and services based on cutting-edge technology. In turn, the way the Internet and mobile communications are employed throughout virtually all sectors of the economy has led to greater productivity in the provision of traditional products and services.

Globalization

Another impact of technology has been to help catalyse the growth of the global economy, beginning towards the end of the 20th century. At this time, technology joined with other social and political developments to enable capitalism to increasingly break down barriers between nations.

With the collapse of communism in Eastern Europe in the late 20th century, coupled with the introduction of market-based reforms in communist China, suddenly additional nations with huge populations were looking to get into the capitalist game. At the same time, nations such as South Korea, India, and Brazil reached stages in their own economic development where they could be forces on the global stage. Finally, developed nations sought to lower trade barriers with agreements such as the North American Free Trade Agreemen (NAFTA).

The growth of global trade was not without its growing pains. With the advent of globalization, a nation's economy became more connected with and dependent on those in other countries around the world. For example, when several Asian countries faced economic turmoil in the late 1990s, the economic impact was felt in Western nations at the corporate and individual levels. Another persistent issue has been the displacement of some industries to nations where workers are willing to do those jobs more cheaply.

Because of these growing pains, some continue to object to globalization. In the view of most economists though,

Many U.S. companies have moved their customer service operations overseas.
The India Today Group/Getty Images

trade is not a zero-sum game: it can add to the wealth of both sides of a trade deal. In addition, when nations have interlocking trade and other financial investments, it creates common interests which can be a force for peace and understanding in the world.

CHAPTER 2

ELEMENTS AND CHARACTERISTICS OF FREE MARKETS

The prior chapter looked at some of the conditions that have helped nurture the continuing evolution of capitalism. In turn, capitalism itself creates several distinct elements that interact with one another to make the system work. This chapter will look at some of those distinctive elements of capitalism.

In addition to personal freedom, private property rights, and innovation, some of the defining characteristics of capitalism include the specialization of jobs (known as the division of labour), a price system, profits, and generally accepted rules. None of these originated with capitalism. They have existed as long as people have performed economic functions. The difference lies in the distinctive roles they were made to play in the free market economy.

Capitalism is society organized as a market, in contrast to society organized as government and subjects. Money, land, machinery, labour, channels of distribution, and buying and selling all work together to form such a market. Some institutions, notably government and religion, stand apart from the market; but they also depend upon the wealth it creates for their well-being. Taxes, for instance, are portions of wealth taken from society to pay for government functions. Directly or indirectly then, virtually all members of modern society are either participants in or beneficiaries of the market system.

The following examines how the component parts of that market system operate.

Goods and Services

Given the great variety of items sold in a capitalist economic system, a distinction must be made between goods and services. In the case of goods, something is produced: food, clothing, cars, houses, and more. Goods are also called products or commodities (though sometimes commodities are natural resources). Services are not products, though services use many products. A motion picture, for example, is a product, but some means of delivering that product are defined as a service. To show the movie publicly is to provide a service that involves film, a projector, and a theater. Customers see the movie but they do not take anything home with them except the memory of the entertainment. By comparison, a DVD copy of the same movie purchased for home use is considered a product.

There is another significant difference between goods and services. Products provide the basic wealth of society because wealth is typically represented by tangible goods. A service cannot be wealth, because once it has been performed it ceases to be. Services can, however, be a signal of wealth because societies that have produced a great deal of wealth, such as the United States, Germany, and Japan, are notable for the variety and quantity of services. By contrast societies that have little wealth will have fewer services available. People in such poor countries can barely afford the necessities, much less the luxury of services—even such important ones as medical care. A society depends on the continued creation of wealth for its prosperity and survival. Services cannot perform this function. They depend, in fact, upon wealth creation for their continued improvement.

Division of Labour

The modern world has a much broader array of goods and services available than was produced in centuries past. In fact, at one time nearly all work was agricultural, just as it still is in poor countries today. As civilizations developed and cities were formed, the role of agriculture as an employer of people began to diminish. Individuals undertook new tasks: mining, handicrafts, trade, and weaving cloth, for example. This simple division of labour paved the way for a greater creation of wealth in a society because it permitted people to specialize in certain types of work, thereby creating more efficient ways for producing the wares required in daily life. Greater quantities of goods, in more varieties and of better quality, were produced for commerce and trade.

In contrast to the earliest agricultural societies, the division of labour in the contemporary world is extraordinary, represented to consumers by the great diversity of products and services available. The division of labour is more clearly evident in the factories that make these products. A look into an automobile plant, in which cars are assembled in a series of steps, will show specialization along a production line: managers have decided which tasks each worker will perform, and they have also determined which production tasks can be handled by machines, and which must be performed by humans.

In large part, the transition from agricultural to industrialized economies was marked by this division of labour, the separation of a work process into a number of tasks, with each

Factory assembly lines illustrate the division of labour, one of the hallmarks of industrialization. Bloomberg/Getty Images

task performed by a separate person or group of persons. It is most often applied to systems of mass production and is one of the basic organizing principles of the assembly line. Breaking down work into simple, repetitive tasks eliminates unnecessary motion and limits the handling of different tools and parts. The consequent reduction in production time and the ability to replace craftsmen with lower-paid, unskilled workers result in lower production costs and a less expensive final product. Contrary to popular belief, however, division of labour does not necessarily lead to a decrease in skills—known as proletarianization—among the working population. The Scottish economist Adam Smith saw this splitting of tasks as a key to economic progress by providing a cheaper and more efficient means of producing goods.

The French scholar Émile Durkheim first used the phrase *division of labour* in a sociological sense in his discussion of social evolution. Rather than viewing division of labour as a consequence of a desire for material abundance, Durkheim stated that specialization arose from changes in social structure caused by an assumed natural increase in the size and density of population and a corresponding increase in competition for survival. Division of labour functioned to keep societies from breaking apart under these conditions.

The intensive specialization in industrial societies—the refinement and simplification of tasks (especially associated with a machine technology) so that a worker often produces only a small part of a particular commodity—is not usually found in nonindustrialized societies. There is rarely a division of labour within an industry in nonliterate communities, except perhaps for the production of larger goods (such as houses or canoes); in these cases the division is often a temporary one, and each worker is competent to perform other phases of the task. There may be some specialization in types of product (e.g., one worker may produce pottery for religious uses; another, pottery for ordinary uses), but each worker usually performs all steps of the process.

A division of labour based on sex appears to be universal, but the form that this takes varies widely across cultures, and divisions of labour based on sex are increasingly diminished in the most advanced economies. Divisions on the basis of age, clan affiliation, hereditary position, or guild membership, as well as regional and craft specialization, are also found.

Industrialization

Industrialization is the process of converting to a socioeconomic order in which industry is dominant.

How or why some agrarian societies have evolved into industrial states is not always fully understood. What is certainly known, though, is that the changes that took place in Britain during the Industrial Revolution of the late 18th and 19th centuries provided a prototype for the early industrializing nations of Western Europe and North America. Along with its technological components (e.g., the mechanization of labour and the reliance upon inanimate sources of energy), the process of industrialization entailed profound social developments. The freeing of the labourer from feudal and customary obligations created a free market in labour, with a pivotal role for a specific social type, the entrepreneur. Cities drew large numbers of people off the land, massing workers in the new industrial towns and factories.

Later industrializers attempted to manipulate some of these elements. The Soviet Union, for instance, industrialized largely on the basis of forced labour and eliminated the entrepreneur, while in Japan strong state involvement stimulated and sustained the entrepreneur's role. Other states, notably Denmark and New Zealand, industrialized primarily by commercializing and mechanizing agriculture.

Although urban-industrial life offers unprecedented opportunities for individual mobility and personal freedom, it can exact high social and psychological tolls. Such various observers as Karl Marx and Émile Durkheim cited the "alienation" and "anomie" of individual workers faced by seemingly meaningless tasks and rapidly altering goals. The fragmentation of the extended family and community tended to isolate individuals and to countervail traditional values. By the very mechanism of growth, industrialism appears to create a new strain of poverty, whose victims for a variety of reasons are unable to compete according to the rules of the industrial

(continued on the next page)

order. In the major industrialized nations of the late 20th century, such developments as automated technology, an expanding service sector, and increasing suburbanization signalled what some observers called the emergence of a postindustrial society.

Labour

While the division of labour can make production more efficient, ultimately the provision of goods and services depends on the availability of labour. In economics, labour is the general body of wage earners. It is in this sense, for example, that one speaks of "organized labour." In a more special and technical sense, however, labour means any valuable service rendered by a human agent in the production of wealth, other than accumulating and providing capital or assuming the risks that are a normal part of business undertakings. It includes the services of manual labourers, but it covers many other kinds of services as well.

It is not synonymous with toil or exertion, and it has only a remote relation to "work done" in the physical or physiological senses. The application of the physical energies of people to the work of production is, of course, an element in labour, but skill and self-direction, within a larger or smaller sphere, are also elements.

A characteristic of all labour is that it uses time, in the specific sense that it consumes some part of the short days and years of human life. Another common characteristic is that, unlike play, it is not generally a sufficient end in itself but is performed for the sake of its product or, in modern economic life, for the sake of a claim to a share of the aggregate product of the community's industry. Even the labourer who finds his chief pleasure in his work commonly tries to sell services or products for the best price that he can get.

If labour could be measured adequately in simple homogeneous units of time, such as labour-hours, the problems of economics would be considerably simplified. But labourers differ in the amount and character of their training, in their degree of skill, intelligence, and capacity to direct their own work or the work of others, and in the other special aptitudes that they require. Tasks differ in their irksomeness, in the prospects that they offer for permanent employment and advancement, in the social status associated with them, and in other characteristics that make one task more attractive than another. Apart from the circumstances that the mobility of labour is imperfect and that it cannot be transferred readily to the employments in which its products have the highest value, the wages of different kinds of labour cannot be taken to be payments for larger or smaller "quantities of labour." The price per unit of time that a particular kind of labour commands in the market depends not only upon the technical efficiency of the labourer but also upon the demand for the particular services that he is able to furnish, upon their relative scarcity, and upon the supply of other productive agents. Thus, the attempts of the earlier economists and of some socialists to find a simple and direct relation between the value of a product and the quantity of labour that it embodies proved fruitless.

Different uses of the available supply of labour, whatever its composition, can be compared with reference to the quantity and the value of the product that they yield. Such comparisons are made continuously in the planning and management of competitive business undertakings. By means of economic analysis, it is often possible to know whether a proposed change in the organization of the community's labour or in the uses to which it is put (as, for example, by encouraging certain types of industries at the expense of others) would be more likely to increase or to decrease the annual production of wealth. For the individual worker, as well as for the community as a whole, the practicable way of measuring the "labour costs" of production is by reference to the other products that might have been secured by means of the same labour or by reference to alternative uses of the time given to labour.

The Market

Using labour and various means of production to provide a product or service is just the beginning. The ultimate goal is to realize a greater value for that product or service than it cost to create. This is done via a market, which in economic terms is a means by which the exchange of goods and services takes place as a result of buyers and sellers being in contact with one another, either directly or through mediating agents or institutions.

Markets in the most literal and immediate sense are places in which things are bought and sold. In the modern industrial system, however, the market is not a place; it has expanded to include the whole geographical area in which sellers compete with each other for customers. Alfred Marshall, whose Principles of Economics (first published in 1890) was for a long time an authority for English-speaking economists, based his definition of the market on that of the French economist A. Cournot:

> Economists understand by the term Market, not any particular market place in which things are bought and sold, but the whole of any region in which buyers and sellers are in such free intercourse with one another that the prices of the same goods tend to equality easily and quickly.

To this Marshall added:

> The more nearly perfect a market is, the stronger
> is the tendency for the same price to be paid for the
> same thing at the same time in all parts of the market.

The concept of the market as defined above has to do
primarily with more or less standardized commodities, for
example, wool or automobiles. The word market is also used
in contexts such as the market for real estate or for old mas-
ters; and there is the "labour market," although a contract to
work for a certain wage differs from a sale of goods. There is
a connecting idea in all of these various usages—namely, the
interplay of supply and demand.

Most markets consist of groups of intermediaries between
the first seller of a commodity and the final buyer. There are all
kinds of intermediaries, from the brokers in the great produce
exchanges down to the village grocer. They may be mere dealers
with no equipment but a telephone, or they may provide storage and perform important services of grading, packaging, and
so on. In general, the function of a market is to collect products
from scattered sources and channel them to scattered outlets.
From the point of view of the seller, dealers channel the demand
for his product; from the point of view of the buyer, they bring
supplies within his reach.

There are two main types of markets for products, in
which the forces of supply and demand operate quite differently, with some overlapping and borderline cases. In the
first, the producer offers his goods and takes whatever price
they will command; in the second, the producer sets his price
and sells as much as the market will take. In addition, along
with the growth of trade in goods, there has been a proliferation of financial markets, including securities exchanges and
money markets.

The various components discussed in this chapter have worked together to establish a society (even on a global scale) connected by an intricate network of market relationships. This market system was unplanned. It evolved slowly, as did the rules by which it operates. The market is a product of spontaneous human action but not human design. People, impelled by nature to maximize their well-being, created what proved to be workable arrangements that augmented individual and social prosperity. The market system does not depend on people sharing the same values, belonging to the same ethnic group, or having the same religion. It does not even depend on their liking each other. It is rooted only in the common desire to improve the material conditions of one's life.

Supply and Demand

Markets operate on principles of supply and demand, which in economics, define the relationship between the quantity of a commodity that producers wish to sell at various prices and the quantity that consumers wish to buy. It is the main model of price determination used in economic theory. The price of a commodity is determined by the interaction of supply and demand in a market. The resulting price is referred to as the equilibrium price and represents an agreement between producers and consumers of the good. In equilibrium the quantity of a good supplied by producers equals the quantity demanded by consumers.

In reviewing the following models that attempt to explain how supply and demand operate, it is important to recognize that these models are theoretical simplifications of very complex real-world relationships. That is to say, there are almost always complications to the supply and demand relationship, but learning the basic principles is a good place for starting to understand how these forces relate to each other in a market.

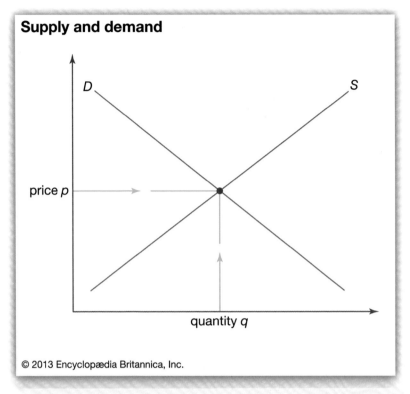

Supply and demand

price *p*

quantity *q*

© 2013 Encyclopædia Britannica, Inc.

Illustration of the relationship of price to supply (S) and demand (D).
Encyclopædia Britannica, Inc.

Demand Curve

The quantity of a commodity demanded depends on the price of that commodity and potentially on many other factors, such as the prices of other commodities, the incomes and preferences of consumers, and seasonal effects. In basic economic analysis, all factors except the price of the commodity are often held constant; the analysis then involves examining the relationship between various price levels and the maximum quantity that would potentially be purchased by consumers at each of those prices. The price-quantity combinations may be plotted on a curve, known as a demand

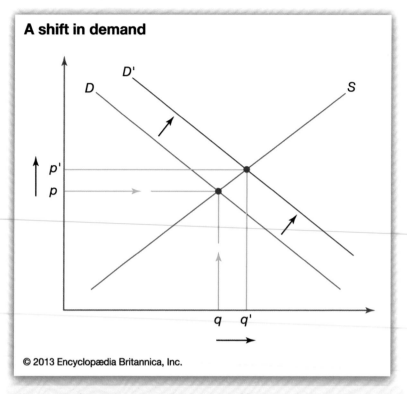

A shift in demand

© 2013 Encyclopædia Britannica, Inc.

Illustration of an increase in equilibrium price (p) and equilibrium quantity (q) due to a shift in demand (D). Encyclopædia Britannica, Inc.

curve, with price represented on the vertical axis and quantity represented on the horizontal axis. A demand curve is almost always downward-sloping, reflecting the willingness of consumers to purchase more of the commodity at lower price levels. Any change in non-price factors would cause a shift in the demand curve, whereas changes in the price of the commodity can be traced along a fixed demand curve.

Supply Curve

The quantity of a commodity that is supplied in the market depends not only on the price obtainable for the commodity

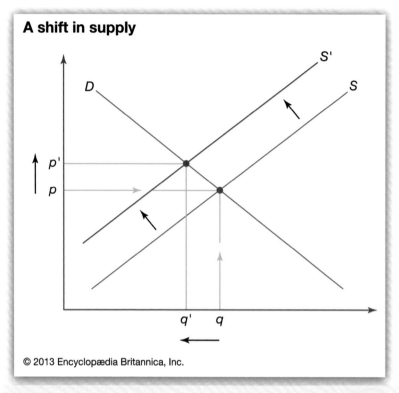

A shift in supply

Illustration of an increase in equilibrium price (p) and a decrease in equilibrium quantity (q) due to a shift in supply (S). Encyclopædia Britannica, Inc.

but also on potentially many other factors, such as the prices of substitute products, the production technology, and the availability and cost of labour and other factors of production. In basic economic analysis, analyzing supply involves looking at the relationship between various prices and the quantity potentially offered by producers at each price, again holding constant all other factors that could influence the price. Those price-quantity combinations may be plotted on a curve, known as a supply curve, with price represented on the vertical axis and quantity represented on the horizontal axis. A supply curve is usually upward-sloping, reflecting the willingness of producers to sell more of the commodity they produce in a market with higher prices. Any change in non-price factors would cause a shift in the supply curve, whereas changes in the price of the commodity can be traced along a fixed supply curve.

Market Equilibrium

It is the function of a market to equate demand and supply through the price mechanism. If buyers wish to purchase more of a good than is available at the prevailing price, they will tend to bid the price up. If they wish to purchase less than is available at the prevailing price, suppliers will bid prices down. Thus, there is a tendency to move toward the equilibrium price. That tendency is known as the market mechanism, and the resulting balance between supply and demand is called a market equilibrium.

As the price rises, the quantity offered usually increases, and the willingness of consumers to buy a good normally declines, but those changes are not necessarily proportional. The measure of the responsiveness of supply and demand to changes in price is called the price elasticity of supply or demand, calculated as the ratio of the percentage change in quantity supplied or demanded to the percentage change in price. Thus, if the price of a commodity decreases by 10 percent and sales of the commodity consequently increase by 20 percent, then the price elasticity of demand for that commodity is said to be 2.

The demand for products that have readily available substitutes is likely to be elastic, which means that it will be more responsive to changes in the price of the product. That is because consumers can easily replace the good with another if its price rises. The demand for a product may be inelastic if there are no close substitutes and if expenditures on the product constitute only a small part of the consumer's income. Firms faced with relatively inelastic demands for their products may increase their total revenue by raising prices; those facing elastic demands cannot.

Supply-and-demand analysis may be applied to markets for final goods and services or to markets for labour, capital, and other factors of production. It can be applied at the level of the firm or the industry or at the aggregate level for the entire economy.

Competition

One factor that has a profound effect on the supply and demand relationship is competition. If there is widespread competition to provide essentially similar products or services, it is known as "perfect competition." Often, there are some limitations on the number of competing suppliers, with the most extreme example being a monopoly, where there is only one supplier. However, cases where there is perfect competition allow the principles of supply and demand to operate most freely.

In perfect competition, a large number of small sellers supply a homogeneous product to a common buying market. In this situation no individual seller can perceptibly influence the market price at which he sells but must accept a market price that is impersonally determined by the total supply of the product offered by all sellers and the total demand for the product of all buyers. The large number of sellers precludes the possibility of a common agreement among them, and each must therefore act independently. At any going market price, each seller tends to adjust his output to match the quantity that will yield him the largest aggregate profit, assuming that the market price will not change as a result. But the collective effect of such adjustments by all sellers will cause the total supply in the market to change significantly, so that the market price falls or rises. Theoretically, the process will go on until a market price is reached at which the total output that sellers wish to produce is equal to the total output that all buyers wish to purchase. This way of reaching a provisional equilibrium price is what the Scottish economist and philosopher Adam Smith described when he wrote of prices being determined by "the invisible hand" of the market.

If the provisional equilibrium price is high enough to allow the established sellers profits in excess of a normal interest return on investment, then added sellers will be drawn to enter the industry, and supply will increase until a final equilibrium price is reached that is equal to the minimal average cost of production (including an interest return) of all sellers. Conversely, if the provisional equilibrium price is so low that established sellers incur losses, some will withdraw from the industry, causing supply to decline until the same sort of long-run equilibrium price is reached.

The long-run performance of a purely competitive industry therefore embodies these features: (1) industry output is at a feasible maximum and industry selling price at a feasible minimum; (2) all production is undertaken at minimum attainable average costs, since competition forces them down; and (3) income distribution is not influenced by the receipt of any excess profits by sellers.

This performance has often been applauded as ideal from the standpoint of general economic welfare. But the applause, for several reasons, should not be unqualified. Perfect competition is truly ideal only if all or most industries in the economy are purely competitive and if in addition there is free and easy mobility of productive factors among industries. Otherwise, the relative outputs of different industries will not be such as to maximize consumer satisfaction. There is also some question whether producers in purely competitive industries will generally earn enough to plow back some of their earnings into improved equipment and thus maintain a satisfactory rate of technological progress. Innovation would effectively be discouraged. Finally, some purely competitive industries have been afflicted with what has been called destructive competition. Examples have been seen in the coal and steel industries, some agricultural industries, and the automotive industry. For some historical reason, such an industry accumulates excess capacity to the point where sellers suffer chronic losses, and the situation is not corrected by the exit of people and resources from the industry. The invisible hand of the market works too slowly for society to accept. In some cases, notably in agriculture, government has intervened to restrict supply or raise prices. Leaving these qualifications aside, however, the market performance of perfect competition furnishes some sort of a standard to which the performance of industries of different structure may be compared.

Price Systems

Whether there is perfect competition or not, the relationship between supply and demand often centers on price. A "price system," is a means of organizing economic activity. It does this primarily by coordinating the decisions of consumers, producers, and owners of productive resources. Millions of economic agents who have no direct communication with each other are led by the price system to supply each other's wants. In a modern economy the price system enables a consumer to buy a product he has never previously purchased, produced by a firm of whose existence he is unaware, which is operating with funds partially obtained from his own savings.

Prices are an expression of the consensus on the values of different things, and every society that permits exchanges between people has prices. Because prices are expressed in terms of a widely acceptable commodity, they permit a ready comparison of the comparative values of various commodities—if shoes are $15 per pair and bread 30 cents per loaf, a pair of shoes is worth 50 loaves of bread. The price of anything is its value in exchange for a commodity of wide acceptability: the price of an automobile may be some 50 ounces of gold or 25 pieces of paper currency.

A system of prices exists because individual prices are related to each other. If, for example, copper rods cost 40 cents a pound and the process of drawing a rod into wire costs 25 cents a pound, then it will be profitable to produce wire from a copper rod if its price exceeds 65 cents. Conversely, it will be unprofitable to produce wire if its price falls below 65 cents. Competition will hold the price of wire about 25 cents per pound above that of rods. A variety of such economic forces tie the entire structure of prices together.

The system of prices can be arranged to reward or penalize any kind of activity. Society discourages the production of electric shoestring-tying machines by the simple expedient of making such a machine's attainable selling price less than the prices of the resources necessary to produce it. Society stimulates people of great athletic promise to learn golf (rather than polo or cricket) by awarding significant prizes (= prices) to tournament winners. The air in many cities is dirty because no one is charged a price for polluting it and no one can pay a price for having it cleaned.

Profit

In trying to meet the demands of the marketplace, the motivation of suppliers is profit. Profit, in business usage, is the excess of total revenue over total cost during a specific period of time. In economics, profit is the excess over the returns to capital, land, and labour (interest, rent, and wages). To the economist, much of what is classified in business usage as profit consists of the implicit wages of manager-owners, the implicit rent on land owned by the firm, and the implicit interest on the capital invested by the firm's owners. In conditions of competitive equilibrium, "pure" profit would not exist because the competitive market would cause the rates of return to capital, land, and labour to rise until they exhausted the total value of the product. Should profits emerge in any field of production, the resulting increase in output would cause price declines that would eventually squeeze out profits.

The real world is never one of complete competitive equilibrium, though, and the theory recognizes that profits arise for several reasons. First, the innovator who introduces a new technique can produce at a cost below the market price and thus earn entrepreneurial profits. Secondly, changes in consumer tastes may cause revenues of some firms to increase, giving rise to what are often called windfall profits. The third type of profit is monopoly profit, which occurs when a firm restricts output so as to prevent prices from falling to the level of costs. The first two types of profit result from relaxing the usual theoretical assumptions of unchanging consumer tastes and states of technology. The third type accompanies the violation of perfect competition.

Rules

Order is brought to the economy by the price system and by rules that everyone agrees upon. Some rules are common to society: for example, no theft or fraud shall be permitted, nor will any transactions involve illegal goods or services. In an increasingly complex economic system, other requirements, such as licensing, certification, or proof of citizenship, will limit access to the market. Many transactions are also guided by the rules of contract. Contracts are voluntary (but legally binding) agreements entered into by two or more individuals. They normally specify the performance of some work or delivery of specific goods at a certain time. A contract therefore is a set of promises signed by the parties to it. As such, a contract has the force of law; and there is a whole branch of law devoted to contracts. The establishment and recognition of property rights also play a major role in ordering an economy. Of increasing importance is the recognition of intellectual property—intangible items that represent great value to their owners. Copyrights and trademarks represent a form of property, for example, because they are signs of ownership. Property rights can also be infringed by counterfeiting and forgery, and by copyright and trademark infringement.

Money

The market relationships described so far are based on the assumption that buyers have something of value to exchange for obtaining goods and services from sellers. While there are barter systems in which goods or services are exchanged by both parties, most often a good or service is exchanged in return for money. Money is a commodity accepted by general consent as a medium of economic exchange. It is the medium in which prices and values are expressed; as currency, it circulates anonymously from person to person and country to country, thus facilitating trade, and it is the principal measure of wealth.

The early 20th century was the great era of the international gold standard, meaning that the value of money was based on gold. Gold coins circulated in most of the world; paper money, whether issued by private banks or by governments, was convertible on demand into gold coins or gold bullion at an official price (with perhaps the addition of a

The value of money was once based on gold. During the 20th century, the gold standard was replaced by a system in which each nation's government backs the value of its currency. National Geographic/SuperStock

small fee), while bank deposits were convertible into either gold coin or paper currency that was itself convertible into gold. In a few countries a minor variant prevailed—the so-called gold exchange standard, under which a country's reserves included not only gold but also currencies of other countries that were convertible into gold. Currencies were exchanged at a fixed price into the currency of another country (usually the British pound sterling) that was itself convertible into gold.

The prevalence of the gold standard meant that there was, in effect, a single world money called by different names in different countries. A U.S. dollar, for example, was defined as 23.22 grains of pure gold (25.8 grains of gold 9/10 fine). A British pound sterling was defined as 113.00 grains of pure gold (123.274 grains of gold 11/12 fine). Accordingly, 1 British pound equaled 4.8665 U.S. dollars (113.00/23.22) at the official parity. The actual exchange rate could deviate from this value only by an amount that corresponded to the cost of shipping gold. If the price of the pound sterling in terms of dollars greatly exceeded this parity price in the foreign exchange market, someone in New York City who had a debt to pay in London might find that, rather than buying the needed pounds on the market, it was cheaper to get gold for dollars at a bank or from the U.S. subtreasury, ship the gold to London, and get pounds for the gold from the Bank of England. The potential for such an exchange set an upper limit to the exchange rate. Similarly, the cost of shipping gold from Britain to the United States set a lower limit. These limits were known as the gold points.

Under such an international gold standard, the quantity of money in each country was determined by an adjustment process known as the price-specie-flow adjustment mechanism. This process, analyzed by 18th- and 19th-century economists such as David Hume, John Stuart Mill, and Henry Thornton, occurred as follows: a rise in a particular country's quantity of money would tend to raise prices in that country relative to prices in other countries. This rise in prices would consequently discourage exports while encouraging imports. The decreased supply of foreign currency (from the sale of fewer exports) plus the increased demand for foreign currency (to pay for imports) would tend to raise the price of foreign currency in terms of domestic currency. As soon as this price hit the upper gold point, gold would be shipped out of the country to other countries. The decline in the amount of gold would produce in turn a reduction in the total amount of money because banks and government institutions, seeing their gold reserves decline, would want to protect themselves against further demands by reducing the claims against gold that were outstanding. This would tend to lower prices at home. The influx of gold abroad would have the opposite effect, increasing the quantity of money there and raising prices. These adjustments would continue until the gold flow ceased or was reversed.

Precisely the same mechanism operates within a unified currency area. That mechanism determines how much money there is in Illinois compared with how much there is in other U.S. states or how much there is in Wales compared with how much there is in other parts of the United Kingdom. Because the gold standard was so prevalent in the early 20th century, most of the commercial world operated as a unified currency area. One advantage of such widespread adherence to the gold standard was its ability to limit a national government's power to engage in irresponsible monetary expansion.

On the other hand, the gold standard was also limiting to the economic policies of nations, and was based on the outdated assumption that gold was the ultimate measure of economic value. Therefore, as the 20th century progressed, the world transitioned away from the gold standard, and towards a system where currencies from one nation can be freely exchanged with those from other nations, with the value of each currency backed by its issuing government. In essence, this more flexible system recognizes that money is exchangeable for an almost infinite range of goods and services, and therefore its value is not solely defined by how much gold it can buy.

Interest

While money can be used to purchase goods, a person does not always have enough currency on hand to make a purchase. For example, most people could not afford to pay cash for a house. People also prefer to carry credit cards rather than travel with wads of paper money stuffed into their wallets. In these cases, people borrow money to make those purchases, and they are charged interest for this privilege. Interest is the price paid for the use of credit or money. It may be expressed either in money terms or as a rate of payment.

Interest may also be viewed as the income derived from the possession of contractual promises from others to pay sums in the future. The question may be asked, "What is the value today of a promise to pay $100 a year from now?" If the answer is $100, then no interest income is generated. Most people, however, would require an inducement to give up $100 today and for the next year. If $5 were sufficient inducement—that is, if they would buy such a promise for $95—then interest income of $5 has been generated at a rate of just over 5 percent.

Various theories have been developed to account for and justify interest. Among the better known are the time-preference theory of the Austrian, or Marginalist, school of economists, according to which interest is the inducement to engage in time-consuming but more productive activities, and the liquidity-preference theory developed by J.M. Keynes, according to which interest is the inducement to sacrifice a desired degree of liquidity for a nonliquid contractual obligation. It may be mentioned that in Marxist theory interest, like capital itself, is a portion of labour expropriated by the capitalist class by virtue of its political power.

Capital Markets

While a person or a business can borrow money from a bank or a credit card company, to handle the huge volume of lending that goes on among corporations and governments there are markets which link investors willing to provide money—at a cost—with organizations looking to borrow money. These are called capital markets.

Capital markets are settings in which buyers and sellers of different kinds of capital—foreign currencies, corporate securities, government bonds, bank loans—meet to negotiate prices. Global capital markets are now open for business 24 hours a day and, thanks to information technologies, transactions can be carried out from anywhere in the world in a matter of seconds. International capital flows now routinely exceed international trade flows by a ratio of 10 to 1. The cross-border integration of increasingly volatile and dynamic capital markets creates obvious challenges for governance.

In contrast to international trade, there is no single international organization to provide governance for international capital markets. In part, this is because there are many different kinds of capital (and capital markets); thus, a central organization would make little sense. However, just as important is the fact that the boundary between domestic and international capital markets has become so blurred that centralized international governance would require substantial sovereignty transfers.

In short, capital markets provide a valuable service as a high-volume, constant source of capital to fund the world's business. At the same time, the investment risk involved in providing that capital can be a source of global financial distress in times of panic.

Distribution Channels

Whether transactions are handled with cash or with borrowed money, buying and selling essentially involves a meeting between supply and demand. Often though, it takes an independent distribution channel to help supply and demand connect.

Many producers do not sell products or services directly to consumers and instead use marketing intermediaries to execute an assortment of necessary functions to get the product to the final user. These intermediaries, such as middlemen (wholesalers, retailers, agents, and brokers), distributors, or financial intermediaries, typically enter into longer-term commitments with the producer and make up what is known as the marketing channel, or the channel of distribution. Manufacturers use raw materials to produce finished products, which in turn may be sent directly to the retailer, or, less often, to the consumer. However, as a general rule, finished goods flow from the manufacturer to one or more wholesalers before they reach the retailer and, finally, the consumer. Each party in the distribution channel usually acquires legal possession of goods during their physical transfer, but this is not always the case. For instance, in consignment selling, the producer retains full legal ownership even though the goods may be in the hands of the wholesaler or retailer—that is, until the merchandise reaches the final user or consumer.

Channels of distribution tend to be more direct—that is, shorter and simpler—in the less industrialized nations. There are notable exceptions, however. For instance, the Ghana Cocoa Marketing Board collects cacao beans in Ghana and licenses trading firms to process the commodity. Similar marketing processes are used in other West African nations. Because of the vast number of small-scale producers, these agents operate through middlemen who, in turn, enlist sub-buyers to find runners to transport the products from remote areas. Japan's marketing organization was, until the late 20th century, characterized by long and complex channels of distribution and a variety of wholesalers. It was possible for a product to pass through a minimum of five separate wholesalers before it reached a retailer.

Companies have a wide range of distribution channels available to them, and structuring the right channel may be one of the company's most critical marketing decisions.

Businesses may sell products directly to the final customer, as is the case with most industrial capital goods. Or they may use one or more intermediaries to move their goods to the final user. The design and structure of consumer marketing channels and industrial marketing channels can be quite similar or vary widely.

The channel design is based on the level of service desired by the target consumer. There are five primary service components that facilitate the marketer's understanding of what, where, why, when, and how target customers buy certain products. The service variables are quantity or lot size (the number of units a customer purchases on any given purchase occasion), waiting time (the amount of time customers are willing to wait for receipt of goods), proximity or spatial convenience (accessibility of the product), product variety (the

A shopping mall is one example of a distribution channel. Bloomberg/Getty Images

breadth of assortment of the product offering), and service backup (add-on services such as delivery or installation provided by the channel). It is essential for the designer of the marketing channel—typically the manufacturer—to recognize the level of each service point that the target customer desires. A single manufacturer may service several target customer groups through separate channels, and therefore each set of service outputs for these groups could vary. One group of target customers may want elevated levels of service (that is, fast delivery, high product availability, large product assortment, and installation). Their demand for such increased service translates into higher costs for the channel and higher prices for customers.

Channel Functions and Flows

In order to deliver the optimal level of service outputs to their target consumers, manufacturers are willing to allocate some of their tasks, or marketing flows, to intermediaries. As any marketing channel moves goods from producers to consumers, the marketing intermediaries perform, or participate in, a number of marketing flows, or activities. The typical marketing flows, listed in the usual sequence in which they arise, are collection and distribution of marketing research information (information), development and dissemination of persuasive communications (promotion), agreement on terms for transfer of ownership or possession (negotiation), intentions to buy (ordering), acquisition and allocation of funds (financing), assumption of risks (risk taking), storage and movement of product (physical possession), buyers paying sellers (payment), and transfer of ownership (title).

Each of these flows must be performed by a marketing intermediary for any channel to deliver the goods to the final consumer. Thus, each producer must decide who will perform which of these functions in order to deliver the service output levels that the target consumers desire. Producers delegate these flows for a variety of reasons. First, they may lack the financial resources to carry out the intermediary activities themselves. Second, many producers can earn a superior return on their capital by investing profits back into their core business rather than into the distribution of their products. Finally, intermediaries, or middlemen, offer superior efficiency in making goods and services widely available and accessible to final users. For instance, in overseas markets it may be difficult for an exporter to establish contact with end users, and various kinds of agents must therefore be employed. Because an intermediary typically focuses on only a small handful of specialized tasks within the marketing channel, each intermediary, through specialization, experience, or scale of operation, can offer a producer greater distribution benefits.

Management of Channel Systems

Although middlemen can offer greater distribution economy to producers, gaining cooperation from these middlemen can be problematic. Middlemen must continuously be motivated and stimulated to perform at the highest level. In order to gain such a high level of performance, manufacturers need some sort of leverage. Researchers have distinguished five bases of power: coercive (threats if the middlemen do not comply), reward (extra benefits for compliance), legitimate (power by position—rank or contract), expert (special knowledge), and referent (manufacturer is highly respected by the middlemen).

As new institutions emerge or products enter different life-cycle phases, distribution channels change and evolve. With these types of changes, no matter how well the channel is designed and managed, conflict is inevitable. Often this conflict develops because the interests of the independent businesses do not coincide. For example, franchisers, because they receive a percentage of sales, typically want their franchisees to maximize sales, while the franchisees want to maximize their profits, not sales. The conflict that arises may be vertical, horizontal, or multichannel in nature. When the Ford Motor Company comes into conflict with its dealers, this is a vertical channel conflict. Horizontal channel conflict arises when a franchisee in a neighbouring town feels a fellow franchisee has infringed on its territory. Finally, multichannel conflict occurs when a manufacturer has established two or more channels that compete against each other in selling to the same market. For example, a major tire manufacturer may begin selling its tires through mass merchandisers, much to the dismay of its independent tire dealers.

Marketing

Whether a company sells its products directly to customers or via a separate distribution channel, it cannot rely on supply and demand to meet by chance. It takes an active effort to identify potential customers, assess their needs and preferences, and present information to them in a way that will influence their buying decisions. Accomplishing these functions is the role of marketing.

A common but incorrect view is that selling and advertising are the only marketing activities. Yet, in addition to promotion, marketing includes a much broader set of functions, including product development, packaging, pricing, distribution, and customer service.

Many organizations and businesses assign responsibility for these marketing functions to a specific group of individuals within the organization. In this respect, marketing is a unique and separate entity. Those who make up the marketing department may include brand and product managers, marketing researchers, sales representatives, advertising and promotion managers, pricing specialists, and customer service personnel.

As a managerial process, marketing is the way in which an organization determines its best opportunities in the marketplace, given its objectives and resources. The marketing process is divided into a strategic and a tactical phase. The strategic phase has three components—segmentation, targeting, and positioning (STP). The organization must distinguish among different groups of customers in the market (segmentation), choose which group(s) it can serve effectively (targeting), and communicate the central benefit it offers to that group (positioning). The marketing process includes designing and implementing various tactics, commonly referred to as the "marketing mix," or the "4 Ps": product, price, place (or distribution), and promotion. The marketing mix is followed by evaluating, controlling, and revising the marketing process to achieve the organization's objectives.

The managerial philosophy of marketing puts central emphasis on customer satisfaction as the means for gaining and keeping loyal customers. Marketers urge their organizations to carefully and continually gauge target customers' expectations and to consistently meet or exceed these expectations. In order to accomplish this, everyone in all areas of the organization must focus on understanding and serving customers; it will not succeed if all marketing occurs only in the marketing department. Marketing, consequently, is far too important to be done solely by the marketing department. Marketers also want their organizations to move from practicing transaction-oriented marketing, which focuses on individual exchanges, to relationship-driven marketing, which emphasizes serving the customer over the long term.

Simply getting new customers and losing old ones will not help the organization achieve its objectives.

Finally, marketing is a social process that occurs in all economies, regardless of their political structure and orientation. It is the process by which a society organizes and distributes its resources to meet the material needs of its citizens. However, marketing activity is more pronounced under conditions of goods surpluses than goods shortages. When goods are in short supply, consumers are usually so desirous of goods that the exchange process does not require significant promotion or facilitation. In contrast, when there are more goods and services than consumers need or want, companies must work harder to convince customers to exchange with them.

Consumption

This chapter has dealt largely with different stages supply and demand go through on their way towards meeting one another, which results in a purchase. However, something critical happens after something is purchased – consumption.

Consumption, in economics, is the use of goods and services by households. Consumption is distinct from consumption expenditure, which is the purchase of goods and services for use by households. Consumption differs from consumption expenditure primarily because durable goods, such as automobiles, generate an expenditure mainly in the period when they are purchased, but they generate "consumption services" (for example, an automobile provides transportation services) until they are replaced or scrapped.

Neoclassical (mainstream) economists generally consider consumption to be the final purpose of economic activity, and thus the level of consumption per person is viewed as a central measure of an economy's productive success.

The study of consumption behaviour plays a central role in both macroeconomics and microeconomics. Macroeconomists are interested in aggregate consumption for two distinct reasons. First, aggregate consumption determines aggregate saving because saving is defined as the portion of income that is not consumed. Because aggregate saving feeds through the financial system to create the national supply of capital, it follows that aggregate consumption and saving behaviour has a powerful influence on an economy's long-term productive capacity. Second, since consumption expenditure accounts for most of national output, understanding the dynamics of aggregate consumption expenditure is essential to understanding macroeconomic fluctuations and the business cycle.

Microeconomists have studied consumption behaviour for many different reasons, using consumption data to measure poverty, to examine households' preparedness for retirement, or to test theories of competition in retail industries. A rich variety of household-level data sources (such as the Consumer Expenditure Survey conducted by the U.S. government) allows economists to examine household spending behaviour in minute detail, and microeconomists have also utilized these data to examine interactions between consumption and other microeconomic behaviour such as job seeking or educational attainment.

CHAPTER 3

BUSINESS AND MARKET CYCLES

At their most basic, isolated economic activities can be thought of in terms of neat little diagrams of supply and demand, but to constitute the day-to-day activity of an actual economy, those activities have to be projected out a million times with a multitude of variables affecting them. In operation then, the bigger picture of economic activity becomes somewhat more unpredictable than supply and demand meeting regularly in an orderly fashion. Sometimes, supply and demand get out of synch, and for this reason, business cycles occur.

Modern economies have alternated between periods of boom and bust. These are times of economic expansion and prosperity followed by economic downturns. Such periods of economic expansion followed by a contraction are called business cycles. During periods of expansion, employment remains high and prices remain stable or rise.

In a downturn, or recession, unemployment will rise, companies may be forced out of business, and prices tend to fall. Such economic cycles must not be confused with individual business or industry fluctuations. A fluctuation of supply and demand, or of prices, may occur in a specific segment of the economy (or in several segments) without severely damaging the whole economy. In a business cycle the whole economy is affected simultaneously, in both its upswing and its downturn. Some geographic areas of a country may be affected more than others, depending on the types of local industries, agriculture, or natural resources such as timber and minerals.

A business cycle usually spans several years. When the economy as a whole is slowing down, a recession is under way. A severe and extended recession, known as a depression, is relatively rare. While the first half of the 20th century is marked by memories of the Great Depression, recessions in that century were far more common full depressions. Between the middle and the end of the 20th century, for example, the United States economy experienced nine recessions. They reached their lowest points in October 1949, May 1954, April 1958, February 1961, November 1970, March 1975, July of 1980, November 1982, and March of 1991. Already, the

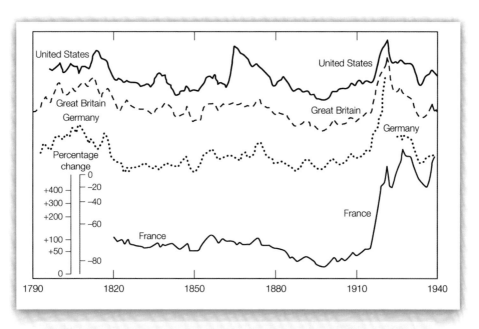

Wholesale price indexes for United States, Great Britain, Germany, and France, 1790–1940. Reprinted from A. Burns and W. Mitchell, *Measuring Business Cycles*; by permission of the National Bureau of Economic Research

21st century has seen two more recessions. The first reached its lowest point in November of 2001, and the second – often called the "Great Recession" because of its severity – reached its lowest point in June of 2009.

Economists, politicians, and others have been intrigued by business cycles since at least the early 19th century. One of the more unusual explanations was proposed by English economist William Stanley Jevons in the 19th century. He believed the ups and downs of an economy were caused by sunspot cycles, which affected agriculture and caused cycles of bad and good harvests. This hypothesis is not taken seriously today.

Most business-cycle theories fall into one of two categories. Some economists assert that economies have basic flaws which, for some reason, lead to cycles. Other economists insist that only some form of outside interference can cause swings from high to low unemployment. Unemployment and business failures are the most visible and characteristic signs of a recession. Those who accept the flawed-economy theory usually insist that economies are far too large and complex to operate without a significant degree of government guidance and regulation. Those who hold the opposite view believe that economies are not inherently flawed and that there will be no business cycles as long as there is no outside interference from governments, banks, or other sources.

A different view was expressed by economist Joseph Schumpeter, who believed that business slowdowns represented a normal phase of the business cycle. In this view, recessions are seen as inevitable and not preventable, and a relatively small negative adjustment in the business cycle is preferable to an economic depression.

All economies undergo stress and shock from time to time. Natural disasters, such as hurricanes, tornadoes, floods, and earthquakes, can do serious economic damage, but the damage tends to be localized. If a severe freeze wipes out the Florida orange and grapefruit crops, the growers lose money; consumers are forced to pay more for these goods, since there are fewer of them. A more severe shock, such as the increases in oil prices during the 1970s or the 2008 financial crisis, can have far-reaching consequences. But economies adjust to the new situation in a few years.

Shifts in the quantity or types of goods produced, minor changes in pricing, and other temporary economic fluctuations do not constitute business cycles. They are adjustments that economies have always endured. But what causes a widespread buildup of prosperity followed by a sudden decline? Since money is the connecting link between all economic activities, the answer must be sought there.

Economies exist because people exchange goods and services for money. This means that economies are consumer-driven. Everyone is a consumer, though not everyone is a producer. Producers spend money for land, buildings, machinery, resources, and workers. Money circulates through the economy as producers pay owners of land, builders of buildings, makers of machinery, sellers of resources, and a labour force. Products, when they are sold, circulate money back to the producers to keep production going.

The money that producers use to start a business comes from investment. Investors decide to put money into a business when they believe that a product or service will have a good chance of success. Some people invest by buying stock, which represents ownership in a company. Others invest by making loans—buying bonds issued by the company. Once a business is operating, it gets the bulk of its funds for future growth and continued operations from borrowing.

Amassing investment money is the start of a process called capital formation. Investment money is the initial capital. It is used to pay for capital goods: the land, buildings, machinery, and labour force. The source of investment money is savings. Saving is postponed consumption—that is, instead of spending today to consume now, some people save in order to be able to consume later. The money available for investment, especially for loans to business, comes from the savings of all participants in the economy—individuals as well as organizations. The supply of money may be a very large amount, but it is a fairly stable amount. This means there is competition for it. Money, like any commodity, has a price because it is scarce. The price is called interest. Money set aside in savings earns interest. Both the interest and the original investment can be used for consumption in the future. If savings exceeds demand, interest rates will be low. If demand exceeds savings, interest rates rise. But there is generally a balance between savings and investment in the normal course of economic activity. In other words, supply and demand in a free-market economy are inclined toward equilibrium.

Businesses borrow money to expand their enterprises based on the money available for loans. They take it for granted that the money available for lending represents an overall consumer preference for future consumption. Guided by this preference, business operators adjust their plans for the future. If, however, their plans are too optimistic, businesses may be tempted to grow too quickly, taking loans for capital with which to build new production plants, hire more workers, and expand into new markets—all sound practices in a growing economy.

If an economy is slowing down, or if the growth in the number of customers a business expects to serve simply does not exist, the company will be expanding unreasonably. Instead of realistic expansion for future needs, businesses are making "malinvestments"—a term coined by economist Ludwig von Mises. These are investments that will not pay off—

somewhat like borrowing to build a factory to make a product no one wants.

The process of malinvestment (or overinvestment) usually takes place over several years. New office buildings are constructed, factories are expanded, machinery is purchased, and additional workers are hired—all to be ready for an anticipated surge of consumer buying power. In some cases, however, the explosion of consumerism never happens. Consumers never voted with their money, by means of their savings, to approve an excessive expansion.

Awareness of this imbalance gradually works its way through the economy. Businesses realize they are in trouble. They have too many workers, too much machinery, excessive inventories, and too much debt. It is time for businesses to work off this excess capacity. So the economy, which has grown like a balloon, begins to shrink. People lose their jobs as businesses fail or are sold. Inventories are unloaded, sometimes at bargain prices, and production levels are trimmed. A great inventory adjustment, called a recession, takes place—inventories of goods, machinery, resources, and workers. This progression is one example of a typical business cycle.

Creating a business cycle has never been the goal of any country or economic system. In fact, attempts by governments to guide and stabilize their economies began early in the 20th century, when, for the first time, unemployment became a political issue. After World War II, the U.S. government deliberately established a full-employment policy to avoid another depression. By then it had become generally accepted by economists and politicians alike that governments could fine-tune the economy through adjustments in tax policy, government spending, and control of the money supply. The writings of economist John Maynard Keynes were extremely influential in spreading this view. Unfortunately, such interventions by governments can also harm instead of help an ailing economy.

Before the end of the 20th century, public confidence in economic management by government had declined worldwide. This occurred as economies underwent dramatic changes in workforce composition, spurred by the information revolution, changes in manufacturing and inventory management, and increases in global trade. Throughout history there have been periods of innovation and quieter periods in which the innovations were absorbed. The world has passed through the era of steam, the era of petroleum, and the era of electricity. It more recently moved into the "digital era," in which computers and the Internet influenced almost all aspects of economic production. In this view, economic fluctuations are not "bad" at all but are, instead, a healthy adjustment to underlying conditions—an adjustment that is necessary if economic growth is to continue.

This view that business cycles are normal occurrences which did not warrant government interference was severely challenged in the early 21st century. In the Great Recession, a real estate collapse, the threat of massive defaults in the financial sector, and a stock market crash triggered a global crisis. Governments, central banks, and international agencies around the world took extraordinary action to address this crisis; while some disagreed with individual tactics used, few argued with the necessity of this kind of intervention to prevent the crisis from getting worse.

Statistical Studies of Cycles

Modern economic history has recorded a number of periods of difficult times, often called depressions, during which the business economy was marked by sudden stock market declines, commercial bankruptcies, bank failures, and mounting unemployment. Such crises were once looked upon as pathological incidents or catastrophes in economic life, rather than as a normal part of it. The notion of a "cycle" implies a different view. There is no one perfect, universally-accepted explanation of economic cycles, but studying different theories can help paint a picture of the different factors that may be involved. The following examples represent some of the attempts theorists have made to explain and predict business cycles.

The Juglar Cycle

The first authority to explore economic cycles as periodically recurring phenomena was the French physician and statistician Clément Juglar, who in 1860 identified cycles based on a periodicity of roughly 8 to 11 years. Scholars who developed Juglar's approach further distinguished three phases, or periods, of a typical cycle: prosperity, crisis, and liquidation. Subsequent analysis designated the years 1825, 1836, 1847, 1857, 1866, 1873, 1882, 1890, 1900, 1907, 1913, 1920, and 1929 as initial years of a downswing (i.e., the beginning of the "crisis" phase).

The so-called Juglar cycle has often been regarded as the true, or major, economic cycle, but several smaller cycles have also been identified. Close study of the interval between the peaks of the Juglar cycle suggests that partial setbacks occur during the expansion, or upswing, and that there are partial recoveries during the contraction, or downswing. According to this theory, the smaller cycles generally coincide with changes in business inventories, lasting an average of 40 months. Other small cycles result from changes in the demand for and supply of particular agricultural products such as hogs, cotton, and beef.

Kondratieff Waves

Cycles of greater duration than the Juglar cycle have also been studied. For example, the construction industry was found to have cycles of 17 to 18 years in the United States and 20 to 22 years in England. Measuring longer-term business cycles involves the study of long waves, or so-called Kondratieff cycles, which were named for the Russian economist Nikolay D. Kondratyev. His examination of the major Western countries during the 150 years from 1790 to 1940 identified three periods characterized by slow expansions and contractions of economic activity, each averaging 50 years in length:

1. 1792–1850 Expansion: 1792–1815 23 years Contraction: 1815–50 35 years
2. 1850–96 Expansion: 1850–73 23 years Contraction: 1873–96 23 years
3. 1896–1940 Expansion: 1896–1920 24 years Contraction: 1920–40 20 years

Only these three Kondratieff waves have been observed. Some students of business cycles have analyzed them by statistical methods, in the hope of finding regularities that are not immediately apparent. One speculative theory has held that the larger cycles were built up from smaller ones. Thus, two seasonal cycles would produce a two-year cycle, two of which would produce a four-year cycle; two four-year cycles would become an eight-year, or Juglar, cycle, and so on. The hypothesis is not widely accepted.

Patterns of Economic Depression and Upswing

Cycles of varying lengths are closely bound up with economic growth. In 19th-century Germany, for example, upswings in total economic activity were associated with the growth of the railroad, metallurgy, textile, and building industries. Periodic crises (such as those outlined in the discussion of the Juglar cycle) brought slowdowns in growth. The crisis of 1873 led to a wave of financial and industrial bankruptcies; recovery started in 1877, when iron production ceased to fall, and by 1880 a new upswing was under way. The recession of 1882 was less severe than the previous one, but a slump that began in 1890 led to a serious depression, with complaints of overproduction.

The year 1890 was one of financial crisis also in England and the United States. The British banking house of Baring Brothers failed, partly because of a revolution in Argentina. English pig-iron production fell from 8.3 million tons in 1889 to 6.7 million tons in 1892, and unemployment increased. That depression might have been less severe but for the international financial crisis, especially intense in the United States, where in 1893 a stock market panic led to widespread bank failures.

The recession of 1900 was followed by an unusually vigorous upsurge in almost all the Western economies. U.S. pig-iron production increased by more than 150 percent during the expansion, which lasted until 1907; building permits more than doubled; and freight traffic rose by more than 50 percent. Prices rose more and more rapidly as the U.S. economy approached full employment.

Deviations from Cycle Patterns

Cycles are compounded of many elements. Historical fluctuations in economic activity cannot be explained entirely in terms of combinations of cycles and subcycles; there is always some factor left over, some element that does not fit the pattern of other fluctuations. It is possible, for example, to analyze a particular fluctuation into three principal components: a long component or trend; a very short, seasonal component; and an intermediate component, or Juglar cycle. But these components cannot be found exactly recombined in another fluctuation because of a residual element in the original fluctuation that does not have a cyclical form. If the residual is small, it might be attributed to errors of calculation or of measurement. On a more sophisticated statistical level, a residual element can be treated as "random movement." If the random element is always present, it becomes an essential element of the analysis to be dealt with in terms of probability.

For practical purposes, it would be useful to know the typical shape of a cycle and how to recognize its peak and trough. A great amount of work has been done in what may be called the morphology of cycles. In the United States, Arthur F. Burns and Wesley C. Mitchell based such studies on the assumption that at any specific time there are as many cycles as there are forms of economic activity or variables to be studied, and they tried to measure these in relation to a "reference cycle," which they artificially constructed as a standard of comparison. The object in such studies was to describe the shape of each specific cycle, to analyze its phases, to measure its duration and velocity, and to measure the amplitude or size of the cycle.

Wesley C. Mitchell. Courtesy of Columbia University, New York

In studying various cycles, it has been possible to construct "lead and lag indicators"—that is, statistical series with cyclical turning points consistently leading or lagging behind the turns in general business activity. Researchers using these methods have identified a number of series, each of which reaches its turning point 2 to 10 months before the turns in general business activity, as well as another group of series, each of which follows the turns in business by 2 to 7 months. Examples of leading series include published data for new business orders, labour productivity, consumer demand, residential building contracts, stock market indices, and changes in business inventory. These and other leading indicators are widely used in economic forecasting.

Dynamic Analyses of Cycles

Coincident with the Great Depression—one of the most severe economic downturns in modern times—the British economist John Maynard Keynes put forth a large body of economic theory that examined the relationship between investment and consumption. According to Keynes and other economists associated with his views, any new expenditure—e.g., on building a road or a factory—generates several times as much income as the expenditure itself. This is so because those who are paid to build the road or factory will spend more of what they receive; their expenditures will thus become income for others, who will in their turn spend most of what they receive. Every new act of investment will, thus, have a stimulating effect on aggregate income. This relationship is known as the investment multiplier. Of itself, it cannot produce cyclical movements in the economy; it merely provides a positive impulse in an upward direction.

To the relationship between investment and consumption must be added that between consumer demand and investment. An increase in demand for refrigerators, for example, may eventually require increased investment in the facilities for producing them. This relationship, known as the accelerator, implies that an increase in national income will stimulate investment. As with the multiplier, it cannot of itself explain cyclical movements; it merely accounts for a fundamental instability that Keynesians thought they had observed.

It can be shown, however, that the multiplier and accelerator in combination may produce very strong cyclical movements. Thus, when an increase in investment occurs, it raises income by some larger amount, depending on the value of the multiplier. That increase in income may in turn induce a further increase in investment. The new investment will stimulate a further multiplier process, producing additional income and investment. In theory, the interaction might continue until a point is reached at which such resources as labour and capital are being fully utilized. At that point—with no increase in employment and, therefore, no rise in consumer demand—the operation of the accelerator would cease. That halt in demand, plus the lack of new capital, would cause new investment to decline and workers to be laid off. The process thus would go into reverse. The fluctuations in national income could take various forms, depending on the characteristics of the economy and the way in which the population allocated its income between consumption and savings. Such spending habits, of course, affect both the levels of consumer demand and capital investment. This theoretical analysis does not explain actual economic fluctuations; it is merely an aid to understanding them.

The analysis can be made more realistic by taking into account three other factors. First, one may assume that although the economy has an inherent tendency to swing very widely, there are limits beyond which it cannot go. The upper limit of the swings would be the point at which full employment or full capacity is reached; the lower limit is more difficult to define, but it would be established when the forces that make for long-term economic growth begin to operate. Thus, the upswing of a cycle stops when it meets the upper limit; and the downswing stops at the lower limit, resulting in continuous cyclical movements with an overall upward trend—a pattern corresponding to the one found in history.

The occurrence of a time lag—the inevitable delay between every decision to invest and the outcome of that investment—provides a second reason for expecting cyclical fluctuations to occur in any economic process. This phenomenon is illustrated, for example, in the relation between the action of a thermostat and the temperature of a room. A fall in room temperature causes the thermostat to turn on the heater, but there is a lag in time until the room warms up sufficiently to cause the thermostat to turn the heat off, whereupon the temperature begins to fall again. The shape of the curve of the temperature cycle will depend on the responsiveness of the thermostat and on the time required to raise the temperature of the room. By making various adjustments, it is possible to minimize the cycle, but it can never be eliminated entirely.

In economic life, there are many such lags between the decision to invest and the completion of the project: between the farmer's decision to raise hogs and the arrival of pork chops at the store, for example, or between prices at the time of a decision and prices at the time the transaction is completed.

Random shocks, or what economists call exogenous factors, constitute the third type of phenomena affecting business cycles. These are such external disturbances to the system as weather changes, unexpected discoveries, political changes, wars, and so on. It is possible for such external impulses to cause cyclical motions within the system, in much the same way that striking a rocking horse with a stick will cause the horse to rock back and forth. The length of the cycle will be determined by the internal relationships of the system, but its intensity is governed by the external impulse.

Theories of Economic Fluctuation

Stepping back from the concept of economic cycles, there is the more basic question of why there are any fluctuations in economic activity at all – if supply and demand tend towards equilibrium, why do they not stay in a straight-line state of equilibrium at all times?

Many explanations of the reasons for economic fluctuation have been advanced throughout history. Even the most rudimentary explanation of cycles must isolate the forces and relationships that tend to produce these recurrent movements. The more comprehensive theories must in addition explain why, during downturns, (1) employment falls and unemployment increases and (2) investment declines by a much greater percent than output.

Agricultural and Climatic Theories

Perhaps the oldest theories of the business cycle are those that link their cause to fluctuations of the harvest. Since crops depend upon soil, climate, and other natural factors that in turn may be affected by biological or meteorological cycles, such cycles will transmit their effects through the harvests to the rest of the economy. The 19th-century British economist William Stanley Jevons thought he had found the key to such a process in the behaviour of sunspots, which seemed to display a 10-year cycle. His naïve explanation could not long withstand critical examination. It attracted a certain interest, however, for suggesting a causal factor that was completely detached from the economic system and one that could not be influenced by it in turn. Agricultural theories made sense in the 19th century and earlier, when agricultural products represented between 40 and 60 percent of the output of advanced economies. By the turn of the 21st century, however, agriculture's contribution to the outputs of advanced economies had fallen to 5 percent or less.

Psychological Theories

William Stanley Jevons. BBC Hulton Picture Library/Globe Photos

A number of writers have explored mass psychology and its consequences for economic behaviour. Individuals are strongly influenced by the beliefs of the group or groups to which they belong. There are times when the general mood is optimistic and others when it is pessimistic. British economist Arthur C. Pigou, in his "Industrial Fluctuations" (1927), put forward a theory of what he called "noncompensated errors." He pointed out that, if individuals behave in a completely autonomous way, their errors in expectations will tend to offset each other. But if they imitate each other, their errors will accumulate, eventually acquiring a global magnitude that may have powerful economic effects. This "follow-the-crowd" tendency is a factor in the ups and downs of the stock market, in financial booms and crashes, and in the behaviour of investors. One can say, however, that this psychological factor is not enough to explain economic fluctuations; rather, moods of optimism and pessimism themselves are probably rooted in economic factors.

Political Theories

Some observers have maintained that economic fluctuations result from political events. Even the imposition of a tax or an import restriction may have some dynamic effect upon the economy. In the United States, for example, some economists have speculated that incumbent political leaders pressure the chairman of the Federal Reserve System to loosen monetary policy in advance of an election as a means of fostering prosperity. It remains to be determined whether such political factors are capable of producing cyclical movements.

Technological Theories

Ever since the start of the Industrial Revolution at the end of the 18th century, technical innovations have followed each other without end but not without pause. For example, cycles of rapid growth and measured accommodation took place after the introduction of the steam engine, the development of petroleum-based energy sources, the harnessing of electric power, and the invention of the computer and the creation of the Internet. It is possible that, if a rhythm could be found in these waves of change, the same rhythm might be responsible for corresponding movements in the economy. But it is equally possible that the technical innovations themselves have been dictated by the prior needs of the economy.

Demographic Theories

Even changes in population have been postulated as a cause of economic fluctuations. There are, undeniably, cyclical movements of population; it is possible to find fluctuations in the rates of marriage, birth, mortality, and migration, but the extent to which such fluctuations may be associated with changes in economic conditions is not clear.

Underconsumption Theories

In an expanding economy, production tends to grow more rapidly than consumption. The disparity results from the unequal distribution of income: the rich do not consume all their income, while the poor do not have sufficient income to meet their consumption needs. This imbalance between output and sales has led to theories that the business cycle is caused by overproduction or underconsumption. But the basic, underlying cause is society's inadequate provision for an even flow of savings out of the excess of production over consumption. In other words, saving is out of step with the requirements of the economy; it is improperly distributed over time.

Investment Theories

The fact that changes in the supply of savings, or loanable funds, are not closely coordinated with changes in the rest of the economy lies at the heart of the theories that link investment imbalance to the business cycle. Savings accumulate when there is no immediate outlet for them in the form of new investment opportunities. When times become more favourable, these savings are invested in new industrial projects, and a wave of investment occurs that sweeps the rest of the economy along with it. The new investment creates new income, which in turn acts as a further stimulus to investment. In 1894 an early observer of this phenomenon, the Russian economist Mikhayl Tugan-Baranovsky, published a study of industrial crises in England in which he maintained that the cycle of investment continues until all capital funds have been used up. Bank credit expands as the cycle progresses. Disproportions then begin to develop among the various branches of production as well as between production and consumption in general. These imbalances lead to a new period of stagnation and depression.

Monetary Theories

Some writers have ascribed economic fluctuations to the quantity of money in circulation. Changes in the money supply do not always conform to underlying economic changes, and it is not difficult to see how this lack of coordination could produce disturbances in the economic system. Thus, an increase in the total quantity of money could cause an increase in economic activity.

The banking system, with its ability to expand the supply of credit in an economic expansion and to contract the supply of credit in time of recession, may in this way amplify small economic fluctuations into major cycles of prosperity and depression. Theorists such as the Swedish economist Knut Wicksell emphasized the influence of the rate of interest: if the rate fixed by the banking system does not correspond to the "natural" interest rate dictated by the requirements of the economy, the disparity may of itself induce an expansion or contraction in economic activity.

Rational Expectations Theories

In the early 1970s the American economist Robert Lucas developed what came to be known as the "Lucas critique" of both monetarist and Keynesian theories of the business cycle. Building on rational expectations concepts introduced by the American economist John Muth, Lucas observed that people tend to anticipate the consequences of any change in fiscal policy: they "behave rationally" by adjusting their actions to take advantage of new laws or regulations, inevitably weakening or undermin-

Robert Lucas. © AP Images

ing them. In some cases, these actions are significant enough to offset completely the outcome the government had hoped to achieve.

Although he was criticized for overstating the connection between human behaviour and economic rationalism, Lucas influenced other 20th-century economists who asserted that business fluctuations resulted from underlying changes in the economy. Historically, according to their view, economic fluctuations have been marked by periods of innovation followed by slower periods during which the innovations were absorbed. Business cycles, therefore, serve as adjustments to underlying conditions—adjustments that are necessary if economic growth is to continue.

Since the Great Depression, many governments have implemented anticyclical policies designed to offset regular business fluctuations. The increasing complexity and diversification of modern economies, however, have tended to reduce their dependence on any one sector, thereby limiting the possibility of boom-and-bust effects resulting from specific industries. This generally tends to reduce the broader effectiveness of anticyclical polices directed at any one industry, and makes modern economies overall that much more difficult to manage.

Monetary Policy

Governments have a variety of tools that they use to try to manage economic activity, including regulations, tax incentives, and trade policies. Two of the most prominent tools are fiscal policy and monetary policy.

Fiscal policy relates to how the government manages its budget. By being willing to spend more, or otherwise inject money into the economy via methods such as tax breaks, during downturns, a government can seek to counteract the general contraction in the economy. However, since even the government's budget is small compared to the total level of consumer spending, the ability to influence economic cycles through fiscal policy is limited. On the other hand, since investment is thought to have a multiplier effect on the economy, governments can seek to have a more far-reaching impact on the economy by managing the amount of money available to the economy. This is known as monetary policy, a term which encompasses measures employed by governments to influence economic activity, specifically by manipulating the supplies of money and credit and by altering rates of interest.

Historical Role

The usual goals of monetary policy are to achieve or maintain full employment, to achieve or maintain a high rate of economic growth, and to stabilize prices and wages. Until the early 20th century, monetary policy was thought by most experts to be of little use in influencing the economy. Inflationary trends after World War II, however, caused governments to adopt measures that reduced inflation by restricting growth in the money supply.

Monetary policy is the domain of a nation's central bank. The Federal Reserve System (commonly called the Fed) in the United States and the Bank of England of Great Britain are two of the largest such "banks" in the world. Although there are some differences between them, the fundamentals of their operations are almost identical and are useful for highlighting the various measures that can constitute monetary policy.

The Fed uses three main instruments in regulating the money supply: open-market operations, the discount, and reserve requirements. The first is by far the most important. By buying or selling government securities (usually bonds), the Fed—or a central bank—affects the money supply and interest rates. If, for example, the Fed buys government securities, it pays with a check drawn on itself. This action creates money in the form of additional deposits from the sale of the securities by commercial banks. By adding to the cash reserves of the commercial banks, then, the Fed enables those banks to increase their lending capacity. Consequently, the additional demand for government bonds bids up their price and thus reduces their yield (i.e., interest rates). The purpose of this operation is to ease the availability of credit and to reduce interest rates, which thereby encourages businesses to invest more and consumers to spend more. The selling of government securities by the Fed achieves the opposite effect of contracting the money supply and increasing interest rates.

The second tool is the discount rate, which is the interest rate at which the Fed (or a central bank) lends to commercial banks. An increase in the discount rate reduces the amount of lending made by banks. In most countries the discount rate is used as a signal, in that a change in the discount rate will typically be followed by a similar change in the interest rates charged by commercial banks.

The third tool regards changes in reserve requirements. Commercial banks by law hold a specific percentage of their deposits and required reserves with the Fed (or a central bank). These are held either in the form of non-interest-bearing reserves or as cash. This reserve requirement acts as a brake on the lending operations of the commercial banks: by increasing or decreasing this reserve-ratio requirement, the Fed can influence the amount of money available for lending and hence the money supply. This tool is rarely used, however, because it is so blunt. The Bank of England and most other central banks also employ a number of other tools, such as "treasury directive" regulation of installment purchasing and "special deposits."

Historically, under the gold standard of currency valuation, the primary goal of monetary policy was to protect the central banks' gold reserves. When a nation's balance of payments was in deficit, an outflow of gold to other nations would result. In order to stem this drain, the central bank would raise the discount rate and then undertake open-market operations to reduce the total quantity of money in the country. This would lead to a fall in prices, income, and employment and reduce the demand for imports and thus would correct the trade imbalance. The reverse process was used to correct a balance of payments surplus.

The inflationary conditions of the late 1960s and '70s, when inflation in the Western world rose to a level three times the 1950–70 average, revived interest in monetary policy. Monetarists such as Harry G. Johnson, Milton Friedman, and Friedrich Hayek explored the links between the growth in money supply and the acceleration of inflation. They argued that tight control of money-supply growth was a far more effective way of squeezing inflation out of the system than were demand-management policies.

Recent Activity

The Fed defines its mission as trying to strike a balance between limiting inflation and keeping employment up. The reason a balance must be found is because these are generally conflicting goals. Whereas a tighter money supply may be used to rein in inflation, trying to boost employment may call for a looser money supply, in an attempt to stimulate the economy. This need for economic stimulus was felt acutely in the wake of the Great Recession, which began at the end of 2007.

A prominent source of the Great Recession was a collapse in housing prices, which followed a housing boom that had lasted for several years previously. Since banks lend money in the form of mortgages to pay for houses, trouble in the housing market soon caused trouble in the financial sector – trouble that was magnified by excessive speculation in mortgages. Given the importance of housing and banking to the overall economy, the United States and much of the rest of the world was soon plunged into a deep recession.

In response, the Fed lowered the discount rate to nearly zero, making it very cheap for commercial banks to borrow money. In addition, the Fed took extraordinary measures which were commonly referred to as "quantitative easing." These measures involved regular, massive purchases of long-term Treasury bonds and mortgage-backed securities. The specific target of these purchases was to drive down long-term interest rates, such as mortgage rates. By pushing mortgage rates lower, the Fed sought to help home owners by making mortgages cheaper, and help banks by stemming the tide of mortgage defaults.

Though the Great Recession technically ended in mid-2009, the economic recovery that followed was weak and inconsistent. As a result, it was not until the end of 2013 that the Fed announced that it was ready to begin tapering back its quantitative easing program—and even then, it reduced that program by relatively small increments.

The Rising Profile of the Federal Reserve Chair

The Federal Reserve is a committee whose chairperson has become one of the most high-profile officials in government. When the Federal Reserve Chair is due to speak, news media, investors, and politicians all pay close attention. Financial markets have been known to rise or fall sharply, depending on what was said. While the average person may know next to nothing about the complexities of monetary policy, by the late 20th century the Federal Reserve Chair had become something of an international celebrity. The following are some of the recent Fed Chairs who contributed to the high profile of the position:

Paul Volcker played a key role in stabilizing the American economy during the 1980s. He was appointed Fed Chair by President Jimmy Carter in 1979, when inflation in the United States had reached a high of almost 13 percent. Volcker was determined to end chronic high inflation, and under his leadership the Federal Reserve slowed the rapid growth of the money supply and allowed interest rates to rise. These policies caused the most severe recession (1982–83) in the United States since the Great Depression, but inflation was brought firmly under control and thenceforth remained low. Volcker was reappointed to a second four-year term in 1983 and continued his widely praised performance as manager of the money supply and controller of inflation. He declined to accept reappointment to a third term in 1987.

Alan Greenspan was appointed by President Ronald Reagan to replace Paul Volcker as Fed Chair in 1987. During the years of his chairmanship, Greenspan became known for his decisive use of monetary policy in steering the economy between the hazards of inflation and recession, and he was given a share of the credit for the longest official economic expansion in U.S. history (March 1991–February 2000). Greenspan retired as Fed Chair in January 2006. Later though, in the wake of severe economic problems that soon followed his tenure as Fed Chair, Greenspan's policies were examined more critically. In 2011, the bipartisan Financial Crisis Inquiry Commission found that Greenspan's failure to curtail trade in securities backed by subprime mortgage loans during the U.S. housing bubble of the early 2000s and his advocacy of deregulation of the financial industry had contributed to the global financial crisis of 2008.

Ben Bernanke was appointed to succeed Greenspan as Fed Chair beginning February 1, 2006. With his strong background in academia, Bernanke represented a clear break from previous Fed chairmen, who had usually come from Wall Street. In September 2008 he worked with Bush and Secretary of the U.S. Treasury Henry Paulson to draft the Emergency Economic Stabilization Act, which aimed to protect the U.S. financial system during the subprime mortgage crisis, a severe contraction of liquidity in credit markets worldwide brought about by widespread losses in the subprime mortgage sector. He later led the Fed in its monetary policy efforts to

(continued on the next page)

address the lingering effects of the Great Recession. While these measures helped stabilize the banking industry, the overall economy struggled to improve, and Bernanke became the focus of much scrutiny. Although some credited him for averting disaster, others claimed that he and the Fed did little to prevent the crisis.

Janet Yellen became Fed Chair with substantial experience in the Federal Reserve System. In 2013, President Barack Obama nominated her to succeed Bernanke as the next head of the Federal Reserve System. There was some controversy surrounding her nomination, mainly because many Republicans believed that she would place too much emphasis on reducing unemployment and not enough on controlling inflation. Nevertheless, in January 2014 she was confirmed by the U.S. Senate by a vote of 52 to 26, the smallest confirmation margin of a head of the Federal Reserve System in history. Her four-year term began on February 1, 2014.

The Fed Chair plays an important role in directing the activities of the organization, and in communicating its policies. However, it must be remembered that monetary policy decisions are made by a group called the Federal Open Market Committee (FOMC). The Chair is just one of a dozen members of the FOMC, and the group makes decisions by voting after extensive discussions. Thus, while the media may sometimes portray the Fed Chair as the mastermind pulling the strings behind the economy, the reality is that monetary policy is much more of a faceless, collective effort.

Even in retrospect, the effect of monetary policy on the economic cycle is a controversial subject. Some argued that the weakness of the recovery despite the Fed's extraordinary efforts demonstrated how ineffective those tactics were; others argued that the economic downturn might have been far worse had the Fed not intervened.

Market Cycles and Business Cycles

Two important economic concepts which are sometimes confused with one another are market cycles and business cycles. As this chapter has described, business cycles involve the ebb and flow of activity across the economy as a whole. Market cycles have a much narrower, but still highly significant, definition. They involve movements in the prices of assets from highs to lows and then back again. There can be market cycles in any type of asset, such as real estate, bonds, or commodities, but the term is most commonly used in connection with the stock market.

While market cycles and business cycles are different, they do have a relationship to each other. The following is a description of how financial markets operate in setting asset prices, and then how market cycles in those price levels relate to business cycles.

Financial Markets

Financial markets are arenas where investors buy and sell various assets, including stocks, bonds, commodities, and currencies.

Given the advent of electronic trading systems, financial markets can now be structured in many ways. Historically, they were physical meeting places in which traders came into face-to-face contact with one another and trading occurred on the basis of prices being "cried out" on the market floor. Today many financial markets have lost this intensely human dimension. Instead, prices are displayed across a network of computer screens, and assets are bought and sold at the click of a computer mouse or without any human intervention at all. In such instances, the marketplace has become increasingly virtual, as physical proximity between traders is no longer necessary for trade in assets to commence.

Despite this change in the physical configuration of financial marketplaces, the rationale for establishing financial markets remains much as it ever was. Financial markets exist as a means of redistributing risk from the more risk-averse to the less risk-averse. Some risk is attached to holding all financial assets because the value of those assets can depreciate or appreciate. The more risk-averse the asset holders, the more they will seek to use financial markets to find an intermediary who is willing to accept that risk on their behalf. This, of course, will not be a costless exercise. An intermediary's willingness to accept a proportion of the risk embodied in an asset will have to be rewarded through the payment of a fee.

This, for instance, is the principle through which money is raised on the capital market to provide the resources for investment in new productive capacity. An investor with cash reserves may choose to invest that cash in an asset that has minimal risk attached to it—say, an interest-bearing bank account, which is an extremely safe asset because the bank has almost a zero default risk. Alternatively, those investors may choose to make their cash available to entrepreneurs via the capital market. Entrepreneurs will approach the capital market to raise additional resources when they have insufficient cash reserves of their own to fund their activities, and they will seek investors to accept some of the risk inherent in their entrepreneurial activities. Investors who make their cash available in such a way will clearly require recompense— that is, a fee—for the additional risks that they are taking, and this recompense takes the form of higher returns than would be available from less-risky investments. The entrepreneur must pay a return in excess of the prevailing rate of interest that the investor would earn from a simple bank account.

Financial markets, then, match the risk-averse with the less risk-averse and savers with borrowers. A smoothly functioning market environment will, in theory, exhibit a symmetrical distribution of risk aversion around the mean, and it will be populated by an equal number of savers and borrowers. In practice, though, the situation is rather more complicated because of the dominance of the speculative motive for holding assets. Following the liberalization of trade in financial assets from the 1970s onward, financial markets increasingly became an arena of speculation.

The textbook financial market allows for unproblematic risk pooling, which leads in turn to an efficient structure of risk management. However, the textbook financial market contains no destabilizing speculation. Indeed, in the classic statement of the case for efficient markets, made in the 1950s, Milton Friedman ruled out the possibility of the very existence of destabilizing speculation. He argued that, to destabilize markets, speculators would have to buy assets for more than the prevailing price in the spot market and sell them for less. This strategy is a money loser, and the continual losses that a destabilizing speculator would make are sufficient to cleanse the market environment of any such actor.

Yet, the speculative trade of assets still dominates contemporary financial markets. In general, investment returns are assumed to be directly proportional to the risks that an investor bears by holding a particular asset. The greater the risks that an investment will not be profitable, the greater the expected returns will be if it proves to be profitable. Speculative positions are adopted in the search for higher-than-average levels of return. Investors would hedge rather than speculate if the returns to the two strategies were equal because hedging is a safer strategy than speculating.

However, in attempting to increase their expected rate of return, speculators must also accept an enhanced risk that there may be no realized returns at all. Far from speculative financial markets following the textbook model of risk pooling, in reality they multiply the risks of holding financial assets, by subjecting the price of those assets to the vagaries of momentum trading. Speculative financial markets do not present investors with a predictable price structure that minimizes investment risk. Instead, they offer a means of acquiring additional risk, via the uncertainties of speculative price movements, in the search for higher profits.

Speculative financial markets tend to function relatively smoothly as long as participants in the market remain confident that the price of the assets they hold represents fair value. However, such markets are also prone to moments during which that confidence evaporates. In such circumstances, a flurry of selling activity tends to ensue. This is triggered by investors' attempts to off-load assets to which returns are unlikely to accrue. But all it does is expose the risks that are embedded in assets that are traded speculatively. A market that is bereft of confidence is one in which there is no escape from the enhanced investment risks associated with speculative trading.

Relationship with Business Cycles

The willingness of participants in financial markets to invest depends on their outlook for the investment in question. When that outlook is generally optimistic, prices will tend to rise, and when the outlook becomes more pessimistic, prices will tend to fall. Naturally, the trends toward optimism or pessimism that cause these market cycles are often based on investor perception of the business cycle. When economic conditions are good, investors are more likely to be optimistic, and when economic conditions weaken, investors are likely to become pessimistic.

While the business cycle thus has an influence on market cycles, the reverse is also true. Downturns in the stock market mean that people are less willing to make investments. When investment capital is hard to come by, it can dampen economic activity. So, business cycles and stock market cycles exert a continuing influence on each other.

Still even though market cycles and business cycles are linked in this way, that does not mean they are always in synch. Downturns in the market can occur during an economic expansion if prices have risen by more than the strength of the expansion justifies, and need to be corrected. Also, financial markets are anticipatory—they are generally looking ahead. Thus, a stock market can start to recover even while a recession is still going on if investors feel that the worst is over, and that prices already fully reflect all the bad news.

Market Booms and Busts

The term "stock market cycle" suggests a somewhat normal and orderly sequence of events, like the changing of the seasons. Historically though, stock market cycles have often been irregular, and can be anything but orderly. The most spectacular market cycles are exacerbated by irrational investor behavior—either excessive exuberance or gloominess. Often, one extreme leads to another.

This type of boom-to-bust behavior dates back centuries. For example, the Tulip Mania was a speculative frenzy in 17th-century Holland over the sale of tulip bulbs. Tulips were introduced into Europe from Turkey shortly after 1550, and the delicately formed, vividly coloured flowers became a popular if costly item. The demand for differently coloured varieties of tulips soon exceeded the supply, and prices for individual bulbs of rare types began to rise to unwarranted heights in northern Europe. By about 1610 a single bulb of a new variety was acceptable as dowry for a bride, and a flourishing brewery in France was exchanged for one bulb of the variety Tulipe Brasserie. The craze reached its height in Holland during 1633–37. Before 1633 Holland's tulip trade had been restricted to professional growers and experts, but the steadily rising prices tempted many ordinary middle-class and poor families to speculate in the tulip market. Homes, estates, and industries were mortgaged so that bulbs could be bought for resale at higher prices. Sales and resales were made many times over without the bulbs ever leaving the ground, and rare varieties of bulbs sold for the equivalent of hundreds of dollars each. The crash came early in 1637, when doubts arose as to whether prices would continue to increase. Almost overnight the price structure for tulips collapsed, sweeping away fortunes and leaving behind financial ruin for many ordinary Dutch families.

In 20th century America, the stock market in the United States underwent rapid expansion in the mid-to-late 1920s. It continued for the first six months following President Herbert Hoover's inauguration in January 1929. The prices of stocks soared to fantastic heights in the great "Hoover bull market," and the public, from banking and industrial magnates to chauffeurs and cooks, rushed to brokers to invest their surplus or their savings in securities, which they could sell at a profit. Billions of dollars were drawn from the banks into Wall Street for brokers' loans to carry margin accounts. People sold their Liberty Bonds and mortgaged their homes to pour their cash into the stock market. In the midsummer of 1929 some 300 million shares of stock were being carried on margin, pushing the Dow Jones Industrial Average to a peak of 381 points in September. Any warnings of the precarious foundations of this financial house of cards went unheeded.

A house in San Antonio, Texas, faces imminent foreclosure in February 2009.
© AP Images

Prices began to decline in September and early October, but speculation continued, fueled in many cases by individuals who had borrowed money to buy shares—a practice that could be sustained only as long as stock prices continued rising. On October 18 the market went into a free fall, and the wild rush to buy stocks gave way to an equally wild rush to sell. The first day of real panic, October 24, is known as Black Thursday; on that day a record 12.9 million shares were traded as investors rushed to salvage their losses. Still, the Dow average closed down only six points after a number of major banks and investment companies bought up great blocks of stock in a successful effort to stem the panic that day. Their attempts, however, ultimately failed to shore up the market.

The panic began again on Black Monday (October 28), with the market closing down 12.8 percent. On Black Tuesday (October 29) more than 16 million shares were traded. The Dow Jones Industrial Average lost another 12 percent and closed at 198—a drop of 183 points (48 percent) in less than two months. Prime securities tumbled like the issues of bogus gold mines. General Electric fell from 396 on September 3 to 210 on October 29. American Telephone and Telegraph (AT&T) dropped 100 points. DuPont fell from a summer high of 217 to 80, U.S. Steel from 261 to 166, Delaware and Hudson from 224 to 141, and Radio Corporation of America (RCA) common stock from 505 to 26. Political and financial leaders at first affected to treat the matter as a mere spasm in the market, vying with one another in reassuring statements. President Hoover and Treasury Secretary Andrew W. Mellon led the way with optimistic predictions that business was "fundamentally sound" and that a great revival of prosperity was "just around the corner." Although the Dow Jones Industrial Average nearly reached the 300 mark again in 1930, it sank rapidly in May 1930. Another 20 years would pass before the Dow average regained enough momentum to surpass the 200-point level.

One might think that modern investors are somewhat more sophisticated that 17th century tulip buyers and stock speculators during the roaring twenties. However, as recently around the end of the 20th century, there was a similar boom-to-bust cycle in Internet stocks.

The year 2000 marked the end of the "Internet bubble," a five-year period when the paper value of publicly traded stock in Internet-based companies rose far above the real earning potential of the industry. By 2005 publicly traded Silicon Valley firms were worth roughly one-third of their market peak—a paper loss of approximately $2 trillion. Economic change of that magnitude had a profound effect. In 2005 there were fewer jobs in Santa Clara county than before the boom began in 1995. Venture capital funding, the lifeblood of Silicon Valley start-ups, collapsed from $105.5 billion in 2000 to $20.9 billion in 2004.

Even more recently, excessive speculation in real estate led to a 35 percent decline in U.S. housing prices from July of 2006 to March of 2012, and overpriced stocks plunged by over 50 percent from October of 2007 through February of 2009.

The highs and lows of market cycles are said to represent the progression of investor emotions from greed to fear. After all, as sophisticated as investors may be, and as much as they make use of quantitative tools, in the end they are humans. As long as greed and fear remain human emotions, there will continue to be market cycles.

CHAPTER 4

TYPES OF MARKET ECONOMIES

Capitalism is a broad term. Beyond the basic notion of allowing goods to be bought and sold, there are many variations of how to implement this within the context of a nation as a political entity. In some cases, different models have evolved naturally over time. In other cases, the model has been highly influenced by how a nation's government has sought to control the process. That control can be well-intentioned, based on goals such as trying to protect consumers, provide for the needy, or enhance competitiveness. That control can also be based on less noble intentions, such as trying to reward favorites or enhance the power of the state. In any case, capitalism can be practiced in a variety of different ways, as this chapter will describe.

Theoretical Extremes

Historically, mercantilism and laissez-faire have been two opposing theoretical extremes that have had a profound effect on how capitalism is practiced. Before examining some of the different variations of capitalism that are practiced around the world, it is useful to start with the theoretical extremes that have influenced those variations to one extent or another.

Mercantilism

A thriving economy can help make a nation powerful, but should building that power be the primary goal of commerce? That was the idea behind mercantilism, an economic theory and practice common in Europe from the 16th to the 18th century that promoted governmental regulation of a nation's economy for the purpose of augmenting state power at the expense of rival national powers. It was the economic counterpart of political absolutism. Its 17th-century publicists—most notably Thomas Mun in England, Jean-Baptiste Colbert in France, and Antonio Serra in Italy—never, however, used the term themselves; it was given currency by the Scottish economist Adam Smith in his *Wealth of Nations* (1776).

Mercantilism contained many interlocking principles. Precious metals, such as gold and silver, were deemed indispensable to a nation's wealth. If a nation did not possess mines or have access to them, precious metals should be obtained by trade. It was believed that trade balances must be "favourable," meaning an excess of exports over imports. Colonial possessions should serve as markets for exports and as suppliers of raw materials to the mother country. Manufacturing was forbidden in colonies, and all commerce between

In 17th- and 18th-century England, Germany, and the Low Countries, merchant overseas traders rose to prominence. Mercantilism was one of the earliest stages of capitalism. DEA/A. Dagli Orti/De Agostini/Getty Images

colony and mother country was held to be a monopoly of the mother country.

A strong nation, according to the theory, was to have a large population, for a large population would provide a supply of labour, a market, and soldiers. Human wants were to be minimized, especially for imported luxury goods, for they drained off precious foreign exchange. Sumptuary laws (affecting food and drugs) were to be passed to make sure that wants were held low. Thrift, saving, and even parsimony were regarded as virtues, for only by these means could capital be created. In effect, mercantilism provided the favourable climate for the early development of capitalism, with its promises of profit.

Later, mercantilism was severely criticized. Advocates of laissez-faire argued that there was really no difference between domestic and foreign trade and that all trade was beneficial both to the trader and to the public. They also maintained that the amount of money or treasure that a state needed would be automatically adjusted and that money, like any other commodity, could exist in excess. They denied the idea that a nation could grow rich only at the expense of another and argued that trade was in reality a two-way street. Laissez-faire, like mercantilism, was challenged by other economic ideas.

Laissez-faire Economics

While mercantilism sought to tightly control economic activity, the opposite extreme became known as the laissez-faire approach. Laissez-faire (French: "allow to do") is a policy of minimum governmental interference in the economic affairs of individuals and society. The origin of the term is uncertain, but folklore suggests that it is derived from the answer Jean-Baptiste Colbert, controller general of finance under

King Louis XIV of France, received when he asked industrialists what the government could do to help business: "Leave us alone." The doctrine of laissez-faire is usually associated with the economists known as Physiocrats, who flourished in France from about 1756 to 1778. The policy of laissez-faire received strong support in classical economics as it developed in Great Britain under the influence of economist and philosopher Adam Smith.

Belief in laissez-faire was a popular view during the 19th century; its proponents cited the assumption in classical economics of a natural economic order as support for their faith in unregulated individual activity. The British economist John Stuart Mill was responsible for bringing this philosophy into popular economic usage in his *Principles of Political Economy* (1848), in which he set forth the arguments for and against government activity in economic affairs.

Laissez-faire was a political as well as an economic doctrine. The pervading theory of the 19th century was that the individual, pursuing his own desired ends, would thereby achieve the best results for the society of which he was a part. The function of the state was to maintain order and security and to avoid interference with the initiative of the individual in pursuit of his own desired goals. But laissez-faire advocates

John Stuart Mill. The Bridgeman Art Library/Getty Images

nonetheless argued that government had an essential role in enforcing contracts as well as ensuring civil order.

The philosophy's popularity reached its peak around 1870. In the late 19th century the acute changes caused by industrial growth and the adoption of mass-production techniques proved the laissez-faire doctrine insufficient as a guiding philosophy. Although the original concept yielded to new theories that attracted wider support, the general philosophy still has its advocates.

Variations in Practice

Of course, no theory is ever executed perfectly in practice, and capitalist economies continually wrestle with the conflict between centralized goals and individual freedoms. The following are some examples of how different economies have sought to resolve that conflict in practice.

State Capitalism

Between the extremes of laissez-faire and social market economies, over time many developed nations have evolved into what is known as state capitalism. This remains based on free market principles, but includes a prominent role for the government.

Even in a laissez-faire system, the state is seen as playing a role in enforcing the rule of law, and as a nation develops and builds wealth, those laws tend to become more extensive and complex. The growing power of corporations has to be balanced by regulations protecting consumers, workers, and the environment. Nations may require expenditures for the common good, such as for infrastructure and national defense, which private enterprise will not undertake, so these responsibilities also fall to the state.

In time, the state's role tends to grow to include providing assistance to the needy and the elderly, and to help manage the progress of the economy. The result of all this is that government expenditures grow to be an increasing portion of a nation's gross national product, a pattern that has been seen in the United States between other developed capitalist nations.

In a way, state capitalism can be seen as government adapting to meet the demands of its people. In the early stages of an economy's development, those demands may be few and simple, but as an economy grows so do those demands. In response, the government tends to grow as well.

Welfare State

One of the priorities that is common in state capitalism is providing assistance to the needy. When this expands to the point where the state plays a key role in the protection and promotion of the economic and social well-being of its citizens, it is known as a welfare state. It is based on the principles of equality of opportunity, equitable distribution of wealth, and public responsibility for those unable to avail themselves of the minimal provisions for a good life. The general term may cover a variety of forms of economic and social organization, and some elements of a welfare state are commonly found in developed capitalist economies.

A fundamental feature of the welfare state is social insurance, a provision common to most advanced industrialized countries (e.g., National Insurance in the United Kingdom and Social Security in the United States). Such insurance is usually financed by compulsory contributions and is intended to provide benefits to persons and families during periods of greatest need. It is widely recognized, however, that in practice these cash benefits fall considerably short of the levels intended by the designers of the plans.

The welfare state also usually includes public provision of basic education, health services, and housing (in some cases at low cost or without charge). In these respects the welfare state is considerably more extensive in western European countries than in the United States, featuring in many cases comprehensive health coverage and provision of state-subsidized tertiary education.

Antipoverty programs and the system of personal taxation may also be regarded as aspects of the welfare state. Personal taxation falls into this category insofar as its progressivity is used to achieve greater justice in income distribution (rather than merely to raise revenue) and also insofar as it is used to finance social insurance payments and other benefits not completely financed by compulsory contributions. In socialist countries the welfare state also covers employment and administration of consumer prices.

The modern use of the term is associated with the comprehensive measures of social insurance adopted in 1948 by Great Britain on the basis of the report on *Social Insurance and Allied Services* (1942) by Sir William (later Lord) Beveridge. In the 20th century, as the earlier concept of the passive laissez-faire state was gradually abandoned, almost all states sought to provide at least some of the measures of social insurance associated with the welfare state. Thus, in the United States the New Deal of Pres. Franklin D. Roosevelt, the Fair Deal of Pres. Harry S. Truman, and a large part of the domestic programs of later presidents were based on welfare state principles. In its more thoroughgoing form, the welfare state provides state aid for the individual in almost all phases of life—"from the cradle to the grave"—as exemplified in the Netherlands and the Social Democratic governments of the Scandinavian countries. Many less-developed countries have the establishment of some form of welfare state as their goal.

Henry Ford developed an internal welfare system for his employees. He believed that establishing a loyal and committed labour force would yield higher efficiency and greater productivity. AFP/Getty Images

The principal problems in the administration of a welfare state are: determining the desirable level of provision of services by the state; ensuring that the system of personal benefits and contributions meets the needs of individuals and families while at the same time offering sufficient incentives for productive work; ensuring efficiency in the operation of state monopolies and bureaucracies; and the equitable provision of resources to finance the services over and above the contributions of direct beneficiaries.

Social Market Economies

Taking the concept of a welfare state a little further is a model known as a social market economy, which pursues free market capitalism as a means of providing for the collective needs of its people. This is characterized by the willingness of the population to pay extremely high taxes in exchange for extraordinarily comprehensive social services. This model is practiced throughout much of northern Europe.

For example, in Norway, direct taxes are high, with sharply progressive income taxes and wealth taxes on personal property. The country also levies a value-added (or consumption) tax of about 25 percent—among the highest value-added taxes in Europe—on all economic activity. Total tax revenues are equivalent to about half of the country's GNP, but much of this represents transfers of income (i.e., it is returned to the private sector in the form of price subsidies, social insurance benefits, and the like). All this has added to economic problems of inflation, but increases in productivity have made possible a high rate of growth in real income. Unemployment generally has been below that of much of western Europe.

Compulsory membership in a national health-insurance system guarantees all Norwegians free medical care in hospitals, compensation for doctors' fees, and free medicine, as well as an allowance to compensate for lost wages. Membership fees securing cash benefits during illness or pregnancy, covered by another insurance fund, are compulsory for salaried employees and optional for the self-employed. There is also a well-developed system of maternal and child health care, as well as compulsory school health services and free family counseling by professionals. A public dental service provides care for children under age 18.

A "people's pension" was established in Norway in 1967 to ensure each citizen upon retirement a standard of living reasonably close to the level that the individual had achieved during his or her working life. The pension covers old age and cases of disability or loss of support. The premiums are paid by the individual members, employers, municipalities, and the state. The basic pension is adjusted every year, regardless of the plan's income. Supplementary pensions vary according to income and pension-earning time. The state pays a family allowance for all children up to 18 years of age.

While some argue that high taxes suppress economic growth, Norway ranks among the top 10 countries of the world in GNP per capita and has one of the world's highest standards of living. The Nordic economic model is followed to varying degrees by a number of northern European nations, and to some extent Germany.

Command Economies

A welfare state and social market economies represent varying degrees of state interference with free market principles in an effort to provide social service to a nation's people. Sometimes though, state interference is more motivated by enhancing the power of the state, as in the case of command economies. These economies have only minor elements of capitalist principles because while goods are bought and sold, the term and conditions for that activity is strictly dictated by the state rather than determined by the market.

A command economy is an economic system in which the means of production are publicly owned and economic activity is controlled by a central authority that assigns quantitative production goals and allots raw materials to productive enterprises. In such a system, determining the proportion of total product used for investment rather than consumption becomes a centrally made political decision. After this decision has been made, the central planners work out the assortment of goods to be produced and the quotas for each enterprise. Consumers may influence the planners' decisions indirectly if the planners take into consideration the surpluses and shortages that have developed in the market. The only direct choice made by consumers, however, is among the commodities already produced.

Prices are also set by the central planners, but they do not serve, as in a market economy, as signals to producers of goods to increase or decrease production. Instead, they are used mainly as instruments of the central planners in their efforts to reconcile the total demand for consumer goods with the supply available, allowing also for revenues to the state.

The central authority in a command economy assigns production goals in terms of physical units and allocates physical quantities of raw materials to enterprises. The process for a large economy with millions of products is extremely complex and has encountered a number of difficulties in practice.

Central planning of this kind is not without apparent advantages, however, since it enables a government to mobilize resources quickly on a national scale during wartime or some other national emergency. But the costs of centralized policies are real and quite high. Public ownership and codified production goals remove the incentives for innovation and individual effort, things which make freer economies more dynamic. In the early 1960s, Soviet Premier Nikita Khrushchev boasted that within two decades, his country would surpass the United States in the production of steel and cement. His country met those goals, but in the meantime American entrepreneurs were creating microprocessors and new forms of telecommunications that would lead to newer, more profitable industries. This is an example of how centralized planning can fail to allow for the conditions that allow economies to make dramatic breakthroughs.

Corporatist Economies

Another example of the state tightly controlling economic activity to pursue its own goals is a corporatist economy. Corporatism is the theory and practice of organizing society into "corporations" subordinate to the state.

According to corporatist theory, workers and employers would be organized into industrial and professional corporations serving as organs of political representation and controlling to a large extent the persons and activities within their jurisdiction. However, as the "corporate state" was put into effect in fascist Italy between World Wars I and II, it reflected the will of the country's dictator, Benito Mussolini, rather than the adjusted interests of economic groups.

Although the corporate idea was intimated in the congregationalsim of colonial Puritan New England and in mercantilism, its earliest theoretical expression did not appear until after the French Revolution (1789) and was strongest in eastern Germany and Austria. The chief spokesman for this corporatism—or "distributism," as it was later called in Germany—was Adam Müller, the court philosopher for Prince Klemens Metternich. Müller's attacks on French egalitarianism and on the laissez-faire economics of the Scottish political economist Adam Smith were vigorous attempts to find a modern justification for traditional institutions and led him to conceive of a modernized *Ständestaat* ("class state"), which might claim sovereignty and divine right because it would be organized to regulate production and coordinate class interests.

The advent of Italian fascism provided an opportunity to implement the theories of the corporate state. Beginning in 1919 Mussolini and his associates sought to gain power through controlling economic activity. By 1934, a decree created 22 corporations—each for a particular field of economic activity (*categoria*) and each responsible not only for the administration of labour contracts but also for the promotion of the interests of its field in general. At the head of each corporation was a council, on which employers and employees had equal representation. To coordinate the work of the corporations, Mussolini's government created a central corporative committee, which turned out in practice to be indistinguishable from the ministry of corporations. In 1936 the national Council of Corporations met as the successor to the Chamber of Deputies and as Italy's supreme legislative body. The council was composed of 823 members, 66 of whom represented the Fascist Party; the remainder comprised representatives of the employer and employee confederations, distributed among the 22 corporations. The creation of this body was heralded as the completion of the legal structure of the corporate state. However, the system was broken by the onset of World War II.

After the war the governments of many democratic western European countries—e.g., Austria, Norway, and Sweden—developed strong corporatist elements in an attempt to mediate and reduce conflict between businesses and trade unions and to enhance economic growth.

Mixed Economies

Economic systems rarely exist in pure form. Even in countries that pride themselves on free market principles tend to have some elements of a welfare state, and often even corporatism and command economies. The reality, then, is that most economies employ a mixture of economic systems, which can create tensions. Those tensions are especially evident in countries attempting to transition from one form of economy for another.

For example, in its later years, the Soviet Union attempted to find a more flexible amalgam of planning and market techniques, an effort that was anticipated by several decades of cautious experiment in some of the socialist countries of Eastern Europe, especially Yugoslavia and Hungary, and by bold departures from central planning in China after 1979. All these economies existed in some degree of flux as their governments sought configurations best suited to their institutional legacies, political ideologies, and cultural traditions. All of them also encountered problems similar in kind, although not in degree, to those of the Soviet Union as they sought to escape the confines of highly centralized economic control. After the Soviet Union abandoned its control over eastern Europe in 1989–90, most of that region's countries began converting their economies into capitalist-like systems, as ultimately did Russia after the Soviet Union's collapse.

Something of this mixed system of coordination can also be seen in the less-developed regions of the world. These economies represent a panoply of economic systems, with tradition-dominated tribal societies, absolute monarchies, and semifeudal societies side by side with military socialisms and sophisticated but unevenly developed capitalisms. To some extent, this spectrum reflects the legacy of 19th-century imperialist capitalism, against whose cultural as well as economic hegemony all latecomers have had to struggle. Little can be ventured as to the outcome of this astonishing variety of economic structures. A few may follow the corporatist model of the Asian tigers and the economies of the Pacific Rim (a group of Pacific Ocean countries and islands that constitute more than half of the world's population); others may emulate the social democratic welfare states of western Europe; a few will pursue a more laissez-faire approach; yet others will seek whatever method—either market or planned—that might help them establish a viable place in the international arena.

Recurring Issues

Not only are there different theories about what constitutes the ideal capitalist system, but there are certain problems or disputes that tend to crop up over and over again in capitalist societies. The following are some examples of these recurring issues.

Crony Capitalism

Though not a formal system of capitalism, crony capitalism is a reality that exists to one extent or another under most capitalist economies, though to greatly varying degrees. Crony capitalism is a system of using the power of the state to direct contracts and other economic advantages towards a circle of close associates, or cronies.

The nature of crony capitalism can probably be best illustrated through the example of the notorious New York City official Boss Tweed. William Magear "Boss" Tweed was a politician who, with his "Tweed ring" cronies, systematically plundered New York City of sums estimated at between $30,000,000 and $200,000,000.

Tweed was a bookkeeper and a volunteer fireman when elected alderman on his second try in 1851, and the following year he was

THE "BRAINS"

Political cartoon depicting Boss Tweed with a money bag for a head, captioned "The 'brains' that achieved the Tammany victory at the Rochester Democratic Convention." Library of Congress Prints and Photographs Division, Washington, D.C.

also elected to a term in Congress. He gradually strengthened his position in Tammany Hall (the executive committee of New York City's Democratic Party organization), and in 1856 he was elected to a new, bipartisan city board of supervisors, after which he held other important positions in the city government. Meanwhile he managed to have his cronies named to other key city and county posts, thus establishing what became the Tweed ring. By 1860 he headed Tammany Hall's general committee and thus controlled the Democratic Party's nominations to all city positions. In that same year he opened a law office through which he received large fees from various corporations for his "legal services." He became a state senator in 1868 and also became grand sachem (principal leader) of Tammany Hall that same year. Tweed dominated the Democratic Party in both the city and state and had his candidates elected mayor of New York City, governor, and speaker of the state assembly. In 1870 he forced the passage of a new city charter creating a board of audit by means of which he and his associates could control the city treasury. The Tweed ring then proceeded to milk the city through such devices as faked leases, padded bills, false vouchers, unnecessary repairs, and overpriced goods and services bought from suppliers controlled by the ring. Vote fraud at elections was rampant.

Toppling Tweed became the prime goal of a growing reform movement. Exposed at last by the *New York Times*, the satiric cartoons of Thomas Nast in *Harper's Weekly*, and the efforts of a reform lawyer, Samuel J. Tilden, Tweed was tried on charges of forgery and larceny. He was convicted and sentenced to prison (1873) but was released in 1875. Rearrested on a civil charge, he was convicted and imprisoned, but he escaped to Cuba and then to Spain. Again arrested and extradited to the United States, he was confined again to jail in New York City, where he died.

Despite reforms inspired by Tweed, examples of crony capitalism can still be seen in the United States in how local, state, and even national leaders sometimes award contracts based on personal or political relationships. In some nations, the practice is even more widespread. While favouring select insiders can be seen as being inspired by capitalist incentives, it is also a corruption of the capitalist model, in that it creates unfair advantages for the few at the expense of the many.

Protectionism

Protectionism can be seen as a surviving remnant of mercantilism, since its proponents feel it helps defend a country's economic interests. Protectionism is a policy of protecting domestic industries against foreign competition by means of tariffs, subsidies, import quotas, or other restrictions or handicaps placed on the imports of foreign competitors. Protectionist policies have been implemented by many countries despite the fact that virtually all mainstream economists agree that the world economy generally benefits from free trade.

Government-levied tariffs are the chief protectionist measures. They raise the price of imported articles, making them more expensive (and therefore less attractive) than domestic products. Protective tariffs have historically been employed to stimulate industries in countries beset by recession or depression. Protectionism may be helpful to emergent industries in developing nations. It can also serve as a means of fostering self-sufficiency in defense industries. Import quotas offer another means of protectionism. These quotas set an absolute limit on the amount of certain goods that can be imported into a country and tend to be more effective than protective tariffs, which do not always dissuade consumers who are willing to pay a higher price for an imported good.

Throughout history wars and economic depressions (or recessions) have led to increases in protectionism, while peace and prosperity have tended to encourage free trade. The European monarchies favoured protectionist policies in the 17th and 18th centuries in an attempt to increase trade and build their domestic economies at the expense of other nations; these policies, now discredited, became known as mercantilism. Great Britain began to abandon its protective tariffs in the first half of the 19th century after it had achieved industrial preeminence in Europe. Britain's spurning of protectionism in favour of free trade was symbolized by its repeal in 1846 of the Corn Laws and other duties on imported grain. Protectionist policies in Europe were relatively mild in the second half of the 19th century, although France, Germany, and several other countries were compelled at times to impose customs duties as a means of sheltering their growing industrial sectors from British competition. By 1913, however, customs duties were low throughout the Western world, and import quotas were hardly ever used. It was the damage and dislocation caused by World War I that inspired a continual raising of customs barriers in Europe in the 1920s. During the Great Depression of the 1930s, record levels of unemployment engendered an epidemic of protectionist measures. World trade shrank drastically as a result.

The United States had a long history as a protectionist country, with its tariffs reaching their high points in the 1820s and during the Great Depression. Under the Smoot-Hawley Tariff Act (1930), the average tariff on imported goods was raised by roughly 20 percent. The country's protectionist policies changed toward the middle of the 20th century, and in 1947 the United States was one of 23 nations to sign reciprocal trade agreements in the form of the General Agreement on Tariffs and Trade (GATT). That agreement, amended in 1994, was replaced in 1995 by the World Trade Organization

(WTO) in Geneva. Through WTO negotiations, most of the world's major trading nations have substantially reduced their customs tariffs.

The Costs and Benefits of Free Trade

In 1999, 50,000 protesters greeted delegates to a meeting of the World Trade Organization (WTO) in Seattle, Washington. The protests started peacefully but ended violently, with dozens of people being arrested. This is one measure of the passion that the issue of free trade arouses.

The protests in Seattle set a pattern for what has become a regular accompaniment to meetings of the WTO and other global trade organizations. The people protesting against global trade in Seattle were a diverse group, ranging from conservatives who want the United States to minimize interaction with foreign countries to liberals who believe global trade encourages environmental and labour abuses.

Notably, this type of protest against free trade has been repeated in other countries. Even people on opposite sides of potential trade agreements agree on one thing: they are against free trade between nations.

The arguments against free trade are many. Jobs can be lost, as consumers choose foreign imports over domestically-manufactured alternatives. Some also see globalization as a way of getting around environmental or labour protection laws: wealthy nations tend to have stricter regulations on those issues, but without trade restrictions companies can simply switch manufacturing to nations with looser regulations and lower wages, and then bring the goods back to sell in wealthier nations. More broadly, some see global trade as part of a sinister trend that puts corporate interests above those of citizens.

Proponents of global trade also have a range of arguments on their side. International trade increases economic activity, which ultimately creates jobs rather than just shifting them from one nation to another. Free trade also lowers prices to consumers – every time a tariff is assessed on imports, it not only raises the price of that import, but it enables competing domestic firms to raise their prices as well. Eliminating artificial costs like tariffs makes things more affordable.

In a geo-political sense, global trade has two benefits. Trading with richer nations helps poor nations build up their wealth, which in turn benefits workers in those nations. Also, trade relationships among nations can help give them shared interests and incentives, which can calm hostilities in times of tension.

There are strong passions on both sides of this argument, so it is poised to remain a prominent economic issue throughout the 21st century.

The reciprocal trade agreements typically limit protectionist measures instead of eliminating them entirely, however, and calls for protectionism are still heard when industries in various countries suffer economic hardship or job losses believed to be aggravated by foreign competition.

Differing Priorities of Emerging and Developing Economies

Different economic systems are sometimes a result of differing philosophies, cultures, or resources. Sometimes though, they are simply a natural function of a nation's stage of development.

Established economies tend to strike more of a balance between growth and quality of life issues, such as environmental

Leaders of the world's emerging economies meet at a BRICS (Brazil, Russia, India, China, and South Africa) summit. © AP Images

protection, labour conditions, and social services. In countries whose economies are still developing, the priorities are simpler—maintain law and order, and pursue growth.

This can cause tensions between emerging and developed economies. Since pollution is a global problem, developed economies tend to favor stricter environmental controls, while emerging economies argue that such control will stifle their industrial development. Activists in developed countries resist trade with emerging countries where workers may be paid what seem like shockingly low wages, while in those emerging countries those low wages are welcomed as an alternative to having no job at all.

As a country's wealth grows, these conflicts increasingly become evident within the country itself. In Beijing, where air pollution is terrible, there is a growing movement to put more environmental restrictions on industry. The same conflict is evident in Delhi, India, where the air quality is reported to be even worse than Beijing's, and yet in India pollution control measures are generally decried as being anti-growth.

This is hardly a new problem. London in the late 19th century was infamous for the smog produced by the Industrial Revolution. The post-World War II economic boom in the United States resulted in rapidly-worsening air and water quality, prompting the creation of the Environmental Protection Agency (EPA) in 1970. Today's most developed economies might criticize some of the practices of their up-and-coming global neighbours, but often their own histories show they went through similar phases of putting growth ahead of other considerations.

CHAPTER 5

PERSPECTIVES ON CAPITALISM

As seen in the previous chapter, capitalism is practiced to different degrees and in different forms by nations around the world. The question of which is the best system has never been settled, and remains a subject of lively debate among scholars, between countries advocating different systems, and within nations as popular and political movements adjust priorities over time.

This chapter will first examine some of the academic schools of thought regarding capitalism, and then show how widely the attitude towards the practice of capitalism can shift within a single country, in this case the United States over the past 50 years.

Schools of Thought

In the formal study of capitalism, many theories have been advanced, and in some cases these theories have developed into schools of thought—ideas which have developed a significant following among subsequent academics and policy makers. The following are some examples of those schools of thought.

Classical Economics

Classical economics is an English school of economic thought that originated during the late 18th century with Adam Smith and reached maturity in the works of David Ricardo and John Stuart Mill. The theories of the classical school, which dominated economic thinking in Great Britain until about 1870, focused on economic growth and economic freedom, stressing laissez-faire ideas and free competition.

Many of the fundamental concepts and principles of classical economics were set forth in Smith's *An Inquiry into the Nature and Causes of the Wealth of Nations* (1776). Strongly opposed to the mercantilist theory and policy that had prevailed in Britain since the 16th century, Smith argued that free competition and free trade, neither hampered nor coddled by government, would best promote a nation's economic growth. As he saw it, the entire community benefits most when each of its members follows his or her own self-interest. In a free-enterprise system, individuals make a profit by producing goods that other people are willing to buy. By the same token, individuals spend money for goods that they want or need most. Smith demonstrated how the apparent chaos of competitive buying and selling is transmuted into an orderly system of economic cooperation that can meet individuals' needs and increase their wealth. He also observed that this cooperative system occurs through the process of individual choice as opposed to central direction.

In analyzing the workings of free enterprise, Smith introduced the rudiments of a labour theory of value and a theory of distribution. Ricardo expanded upon both ideas in *Principles of Political Economy and Taxation* (1817). In his labour theory of value, Ricardo emphasized that the value (i.e., price) of goods produced and sold under competitive conditions tends to be proportionate to the labour costs incurred in producing them. Ricardo fully recognized, however, that over short periods price depends on supply and demand. This notion became central to classical economics, as did Ricardo's theory of distribution, which divided national product between three social classes: wages for labourers, profits for owners of capital, and rents for landlords. Taking the limited growth potential of any national economy as a given, Ricardo concluded that a particular social class could gain a larger share of the total product only at the expense of another.

These and other Ricardian theories were restated by Mill in *Principles of Political Economy* (1848), a treatise that marked the culmination of classical economics. Mill's work related abstract economic principles to real-world social conditions and thereby lent new authority to economic concepts.

The teachings of the classical economists attracted much attention during the mid-19th century. The labour theory of value, for example, was adopted by Karl Marx, who worked out all of its logical implications and combined it with the theory of surplus value, which was founded on the assumption that human labour alone creates all value and thus constitutes the sole source of profits.

More significant were the effects of classical economic thought on free-trade doctrine. The most influential was Ricardo's principle of comparative advantage, which states that every nation should specialize in the production of those commodities it can produce most efficiently; everything else should be imported. This idea implies that if all nations were to take full advantage of the territorial division of labour, total world output would invariably be larger than it would be if nations tried to be self-sufficient. Ricardo's comparative-advantage principle became the cornerstone of 19th-century international-trade theory.

Austrian School

Austrian school of economics is a body of economic theory developed in the late 19th century by Austrian economists who, in determining the value of a product, emphasized the importance of its utility to the consumer. Carl Menger published the new theory of value in 1871, the same year in which English economist William Stanley Jevons independently published a similar theory.

Menger believed that value is completely subjective: a product's value is found in its ability to satisfy human wants.

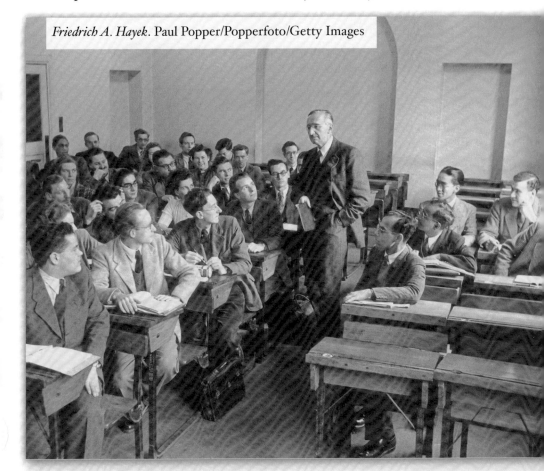

Friedrich A. Hayek. Paul Popper/Popperfoto/Getty Images

Moreover, the actual value depends on the product's utility in its least important use. If the product exists in abundance, it will be used in less-important ways. As the product becomes more scarce, however, the less-important uses are abandoned, and greater utility will be derived from the new least-important use. (This idea relates to one of the most important laws in economics, the law of demand, which says that when the price of something rises, people will demand less of it.)

This theory of value also supplies an answer to the so-called "diamond-water paradox," which economist Adam Smith pondered but was unable to solve. Smith noted that, even though life cannot exist without water and can easily exist without diamonds, diamonds are, pound for pound, vastly more valuable than water. The marginal-utility theory of value resolves the paradox. Water in total is much more valuable than diamonds in total because the first few units of water are necessary for life itself. But because water is plentiful and diamonds are scarce, the marginal value of a pound of diamonds exceeds the marginal value of a pound of water. The idea that value derives from utility contradicted Karl Marx's labour theory of value, which held that an item's value derives from the labour used to produce it and not from its ability to satisfy human wants.

The theory of marginal utility was applied to production as well as to consumption. Friedrich von Wieser based the value of productive resources on their contribution to the final product, recognizing that changes in the amount used of one productive factor would alter the productivity of other factors. He also introduced the concept of opportunity cost: Wieser showed that the cost of a factor of production can be determined by its utility in some alternative use—i.e., an opportunity forgone. The concept of "opportunity cost," as identified by Wieser, is still widely used in modern economic analysis.

Eugen von Böhm-Bawerk developed marginal-utility analysis into a theory of price. Böhm-Bawerk is best known, however, for his work on capital and interest, in which he emphasized the role of time in determining the value of goods. He viewed interest as the charge for the use of capital—a compensation to the owner for abstaining from present consumption. The rate of interest was determined by the size of the labour force, the amount of a community's capital, and the possibility of increasing productivity through methods of production.

The two leading Austrian economists of the 20th century were Ludwig von Mises and Friedrich A. Hayek. Mises (in the 1920s) and Hayek (in the 1940s) both showed that a complex economy cannot be rationally planned because true market prices are absent. As a result, the information critical for centralized planning cannot be obtained.

Historical School

The historical school of economics developed chiefly in Germany in the last half of the 19th century. It sought to understand the economic situation of a nation in the context of its total historical experience. Objecting to the deductively reasoned economic "laws" of classical economics, proponents of the historical approach favoured an inductive method that would encompass the continuing development of the entire social order; economic motives and decisions were seen as only one component of the social order. Members of both the earlier and the later historical schools viewed government intervention in the economy as a positive and necessary force.

Founders of the earlier school included Wilhelm Roscher, Bruno Hildebrand, and Karl Knies, whose works developed the idea of a historical method. They held that the merits of economic policies depended on place and time but that by studying various societies it would be possible to specify certain general stages of development through which all countries must pass.

The later historical school (roughly after 1870) was responsible for most of the detailed historical research for which the school as a whole is known. Its primary founder was Gustav von Schmoller, who hoped to identify cultural trends through extensive historical inquiry. Other prominent members of this school were Georg Friedrich Knapp and Lujo Brentano. Although the historical school was most influential in Germany, its impact was felt throughout Europe and the United States, particularly by the American institutional economists. Because they rejected economic theory, however, members of the historical school had little impact on theoretical development.

Marxism

Before proceeding, it is important to discuss the last of the classical economists, Karl Marx. The first volume of his work *Das Kapital* appeared in 1867; after his death the second and third volumes were published in 1885 and 1894, respectively. If Marx may be called "the last of the classical economists," it is because to a large extent he founded his economics not in the real world but on the teachings of Smith and Ricardo. They had espoused a "labour theory of value," which holds that products exchange roughly in proportion to the labour costs incurred in producing them. Marx worked out all the logical implications of this theory and added to it "the theory of surplus value," which rests on the axiom that human labour alone creates all value and hence constitutes the sole source of profits.

To say that one is a Marxian economist is, in effect, to share the value judgment that it is socially undesirable for

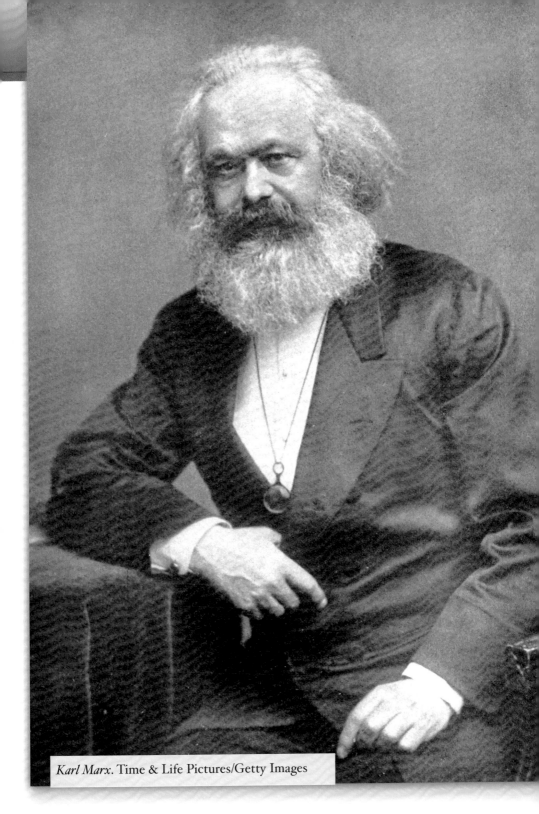

Karl Marx. Time & Life Pictures/Getty Images

some people in the community to derive their income merely from the ownership of property. Since few professional economists in the 19th century accepted this ethical postulate and most were indeed inclined to find some social justification for the existence of private property and the income derived from it, Marxian economics failed to win resounding acceptance among professional economists. The Marxian approach, moreover, culminated in three generalizations about capitalism: the tendency of the rate of profit to fall, the growing impoverishment of the working class, and the increasing severity of business cycles, with the first being the linchpin of all the others. However, Marx's exposition of the "law of the declining rate of profit" is invalid—both practically and logically (even avid Marxists admit its logical flaws)—and with it all of Marx's other predictions collapse. In addition, Marxian economics had little to say on the practical problems that are the bread and butter of economists in any society, such as the effect of taxes on specific commodities or that of a rise in the rate of interest on the level of total investment. Although Marx's ideas launched social change around the world, the fact remains that Marx had relatively little effect on the development of economics as a social science.

Weber's Protestant Ethic

While most economic theories attempt to explain economic systems in terms of people's pursuit of money and goods, there are people who theorize that economic performance is tied to a society's cultural orientation. An example was German sociologist Max Weber, who sought to link economic success to Protestant values.

The Protestant ethic, in sociological theory, is the value attached to hard work, thrift, and efficiency in one's worldly calling, which, especially in the Calvinist view, were deemed signs of an individual's election, or eternal salvation. Weber, in *The Protestant Ethic and the Spirit of Capitalism* (1904–05), held that the Protestant ethic was an important factor in the economic success of Protestant groups in the early stages of European capitalism; because worldly success could be interpreted as a sign of eternal salvation, it was vigorously pursued. Calvinism's antipathy to the worship of the flesh, its emphasis on the religious duty to make fruitful use of the God-given resources at each individual's disposal, and its orderliness and systemization of ways of life were also regarded by Weber as economically significant aspects of the ethic.

Max Weber. Leif Geiges

Weber's thesis was criticized by various writers, especially Kurt Samuelsson in *Religion and Economic Action* (1957). Although English historian R.H. Tawney accepted Weber's thesis, he expanded it in his *Religion and the Rise of Capitalism* (1926) by arguing that political and social pressures and the spirit of individualism with its ethic of self-help and frugality were more significant factors in the development of capitalism than was Calvinist theology.

Institutional Economics

Institutional economics, also known as institutionalism school of economics, flourished in the United States during the 1920s and '30s. It viewed the evolution of economic institutions as part of the broader process of cultural development.

American economist and social scientist Thorstein Veblen laid the foundation for institutional economics with his criticism of traditional static economic theory. He tried to replace the concept of people as the makers of economic decisions with the idea that people are continually affected by changing customs and institutions. Veblen saw the primary motive of the American economic system as pecuniary rather than technological: business enterprise, he believed, was carried on for the amassing of money rather than the production of goods. Another economist commonly associated with the institutional school was John R. Commons, best known for his labour research. He emphasized the collective action of various groups in the economy and viewed their operation within a system of continually evolving institutions and laws. Others often categorized as institutionalists include American economists Rexford Tugwell, John M. Clark, and Wesley C. Mitchell.

Although institutionalism never became a major school of economic thought, its influence has continued, particularly in the works of economists seeking to explain economic problems from a perspective that incorporates social and cultural phenomena. Some see this broad approach as useful in analyzing the problems of developing countries, where modernization of social institutions can be a requirement for industrial progress.

John Maynard Keynes. Planet News Archive/SSPL/Getty Images

Keynesian Economics

Keynesian economics describes a body of ideas set forth by John Maynard Keynes in his *General Theory of Employment, Interest and Money* (1935–36) and other works, intended to provide a theoretical basis for government full-employment policies.

While some economists argue that full employment can be restored if wages are allowed to fall to lower levels, Keynesians maintain that employers will not employ workers to produce goods that cannot be sold. Because they believe unemployment results from an insufficient demand for goods and services, Keynesianism is considered a "demand-side" theory that focuses on short-run economic fluctuations.

Keynes argued that investment, which responds to variations in the interest rate and to expectations about the future, is the dynamic factor determining the level of economic activity. He also maintained that deliberate government action could foster full employment. Keynesian economists claim that the government can directly influence the demand for goods and services by altering tax policies and public expenditures.

Monetarism

Monetarism is a school of economic thought that maintains that the money supply (the total amount of money in an economy, in the form of coin, currency, and bank deposits) is the chief determinant on the demand side of short-run economic activity. American economist Milton Friedman is generally regarded as monetarism's leading exponent. Friedman and other monetarists advocate a macroeconomic theory and policy that diverge significantly from those of the formerly dominant Keynesian school. The monetarist approach became influential during the 1970s and early '80s.

Underlying the monetarist theory is the equation of exchange, which is expressed as $MV = PQ$. Here M is the supply of money, and V is the velocity of turnover of money (i.e., the number of times per year that the average dollar in the money supply is spent for goods and services), while P is the average price level at which each of the goods and services is sold, and Q represents the quantity of goods and services produced.

The monetarists believe that the direction of causation is from left to right in the equation; that is, as the money supply increases with a constant and predictable V, one can expect an increase in either P or Q. An increase in Q means that P will remain relatively constant, while an increase in P will occur if there is no corresponding increase in the quantity of goods and services produced. In short, a change in the money supply directly affects and determines production, employment, and price levels. The effects of changes in the money supply, however, become manifest only after a significant period of time.

One monetarist policy conclusion is the rejection of fiscal policy in favour of a "monetary rule." In *A Monetary History of the United States 1867–1960* (1963), Friedman, in collabouration with Anna J. Schwartz, presented a thorough analysis of the U.S. money supply from the end of the Civil War to 1960. This detailed work influenced other economists to take monetarism seriously.

Friedman contended that the government should seek to promote economic stability, but only by controlling the rate of growth of the money supply. It could achieve this by

Milton Friedman. Chuck Nacke/Time & Life Pictures/Getty Images

following a simple rule that stipulates that the money supply be increased at a constant annual rate tied to the potential growth of gross domestic product (GDP) and expressed as a percentage (e.g., an increase from 3 to 5 percent).

Monetarism thus posited that the steady, moderate growth of the money supply could in many cases ensure a steady rate of economic growth with low inflation. Monetarism's linking of economic growth with rates of increase of the money supply was proved incorrect, however, by changes in the U.S. economy during the 1980s. First, new and hybrid types of bank deposits obscured the kinds of savings that had traditionally been used by economists to calculate the money supply. Second, a decline in the rate of inflation caused people to spend less, which thereby decreased velocity (V). These changes diminished the ability to predict the effects of money growth on growth of nominal GDP.

Changing Policy Perspectives

All of the above theories, and many more, are attempts by scholars, philosophers and economists to explain economic behaviour. These theories are more than just academic exercises. They influence the way a nation's leaders determine regulations, tax laws, fiscal policy, and monetary policy in their attempts to manage the economy.

Naturally, different nations may embrace different interpretations of what makes an economy work. However, even within the same nation, one can witness how changes in the prevailing economic perspective can have a dominant influence on the economic policies of a nation. For example, in the United States, one 50-year period saw a swing from an emphasis on welfare capitalism to a laissez faire approach, and then back to a more welfare-oriented approach. The same period saw Keynesian and monetarist philosophies come in and out of vogue. The following three stages within that 50-year period demonstrate that the economics of a nation are never set in stone or even enshrined in a constitution, but are subject to constant evolution and the push and pull of competing theories.

Lyndon Johnson's "Great Society"

The Great Society was a package of social welfare programs, named for a political slogan used by U.S. President Lyndon B. Johnson (served 1963–69) to identify his legislative program of national reform. In his first State of the Union message (Jan. 4, 1965) after election in his own right, the president proclaimed his vision of a "Great Society" and declared a "war on poverty." He called for an enormous program of social welfare legislation including federal support for education, medical care for the aged through an expanded Social Security program, and federal legal protection for citizens deprived of the franchise by certain state registration laws. After a landslide victory for the Democratic Party in the elections of November 1964, a sympathetic Congress passed almost all the president's bills.

Johnson saw these measures as building on and completing the New Deal vision of Franklin D. Roosevelt; with their adoption the United States joined the ranks of the welfare states of western Europe and Scandinavia. However, the effect of these undertakings was soon vitiated by increasing American military involvement in the war in Vietnam, which eroded popular support for Johnson and created budgetary strains which impeded the implementation of Johnson's social vision.

Ronald Reagan's "Trickle-Down" Economics

Following the so-called "supply-side" economic program he propounded in his campaign, at the start of his first term

President Ronald Reagan proposed massive tax cuts—30 percent reductions in both individual and corporate income taxes over a three-year period—which he believed would stimulate the economy and eventually increase revenues from taxes as income levels grew. At the same time, he proposed large increases in military expenditures ($1.5 trillion over a five-year period) and significant cuts in "discretionary" spending on social-welfare programs such as education, food stamps, low-income housing, school lunches for poor children, Medicaid (the major program of health insurance for the poor), and Aid to Families with Dependent Children (AFDC). In 1981 Congress passed most of the president's budget proposals, though the tax cut was scaled back slightly, to 25 percent.

Reagan's approach was called "trickle-down" economics because the theory was that policies benefitting the wealthy would eventually benefit the poor as well, through the jobs that were created because wealthier Americans had more money to spend.

The results were mixed. A severe recession in 1982 pushed the nation's unemployment rate to nearly 11 percent, the highest it had been since the Great Depression. Bankruptcies and farm foreclosures reached record levels. The country's trade deficit increased from $25 billion in 1980 to $111 billion in 1984. In addition, the huge increases in military spending, combined with insufficient cuts in other programs, produced massive budget deficits, the largest in the country's history; by the end of Reagan's second term, the deficits would contribute to a tripling of the national debt, to more than $2.5 trillion. In order to address the deficit problem, Reagan backed away from strict supply-side theories to support a $98.3 billion tax increase in 1982. By early 1983 the economy had begun to recover, and by the end of that year unemployment and inflation were significantly reduced;

they remained relatively low in later years. Economic growth continued through the remainder of Reagan's presidency, a period that his supporters would hail as "the longest peace-time expansion in American history." Critics charged that the tax cuts and the fruits of economic growth benefited mainly the wealthy and that the gap between rich and poor had grown wider.

Barack Obama's Concern with Income Inequality

In the 1960s, Lyndon Johnson's policies sought to improve economic conditions through policies directed at helping the poorest Americans. In contrast, Ronald Reagan's "trickle-down" approach during the 1980s sought to put more money into the economy through tax cuts, which had the greatest benefit for high earners. By 2014, presidential policy had effectively come full circle to a focus on poorer citizens, and Barack Obama made income inequality a major theme of that year's State of the Union address.

Obama's concern was with the growing gap in incomes between wealthy Americans and those at the lower end of the wage scale. To address this, he proposed policies that would boost the incomes of poorer Americans, such as raising the minimum wage, and expanding the Earned Income Tax Credit.

Supporters of these policies felt that this approach would help lift more working Americans above the poverty line. However, detractors were concerned that raising the minimum wage would backfire because higher wages would force some employers to cut back on the number of jobs. This debate, as well as the sizeable policy shifts the nation had seen over the past 50 years, demonstrates that no one school of thought is universally accepted by economists.

Economic Incentives and Job Creation

Barack Obama's concern with income inequality resonated with many Americans. At a time when millions felt their earnings had stagnated, resentment for high earners was somewhat natural. Movements like Occupy Wall Street were based on the premise that an elite few were benefitting at the expense of the many.

The question is, should the government seek to reverse income inequality? Levelling the playing field sounds like a simple matter of fairness, but taken to its ultimate conclusion equalizing incomes would lead to a communist-style system where there are no economic incentives to do a better job or create new products. In contrast, it can be argued that the opportunity to get rich leads to the innovation and extra effort that makes the economy more dynamic, to the betterment of the many.

Consider the example of Microsoft founder Bill Gates. In 2013, *Forbes* magazine identified Gates as the richest person in the world, with a fortune estimated at $72 billion. Some might question whether one man deserves so much wealth at a time when millions are living in poverty, but the reality is that it does not hurt the average person for Gates to have all that money. If you were to liquidate the Gates fortune and distribute it among all 318 million residents of the United States, it would come to less than $250 per person—not enough to make a meaningful difference in the long run. On the other hand, by having the incentive to amass such a fortune, Gates created a company which now employs 99,000 full-time workers. So, the incentive that benefitted Gates has also created a significant benefit for those 99,000 employees.

In short, income inequality can seem unfair to those at the lower end of the economic ladder. At the same time, a certain amount of income inequality may make for a stronger economy overall.

CHAPTER 6

DEFENSE AND CRITICISMS OF CAPITALISM

As this book has examined so far, capitalism has been practiced in many different forms, and there are even more theories about how it should work. These are more than just technical differences—often, there is a moral element in debates over capitalism, raising issues such as whether it is the best system for the majority of a society, and whether a free society should put limits on how capitalism operates.

Advocates and critics of capitalism agree that its distinctive contribution to history has been the encouragement of economic growth. Capitalist growth is not, however, regarded as an unalloyed benefit by its critics. This chapter will look at some of the arguments for and against capitalism, and then show an example of how the debate over free markets vs. the public good played out in the development of the American economy.

Advocating Capitalism

Supporters of capitalism declare that economic freedom is the most basic of human liberties because it creates greater opportunities for advancement for the greatest number of people. Yet the market system has been strongly criticized by opponents who claim that it fails to provide an equally high standard of living for all. The claim is true: there are and always will be inequalities of wealth under capitalism, but they are not as extreme as the inequalities to be found in other economic systems.

The goal of equality of wealth can only be pursued by force, and governments must do the forcing. An economy itself has no mechanisms of coercion available to it. Those 20th-century systems that relied on force—communism and fascism—failed to achieve a high standard of living for any but a minority. But these are not economic systems; they are political systems. The market economy, by contrast, does not guarantee equal outcomes for all. It merely operates on the assumption of liberty and equality under law for all participants. Success in a free market depends in large part on individual effort and ability, but effort and ability are unevenly distributed among human beings.

Growth

In effect, economic growth is seen by some as the "magic bullet" of capitalism. It may benefit people unequally, but if you add enough growth to an economy, it becomes a rising tide that floats all boats.

Economic growth is the process by which a nation's wealth increases over time. Although the term is often used in discussions of short-term economic performance, in the context of economic theory it generally refers to an increase in wealth over an extended period.

Growth can best be described as a process of transformation. Whether one examines an economy that is already modern and industrialized or an economy at an earlier stage of development, one finds that the process of growth is uneven and unbalanced. Economic historians have attempted to develop a theory of stages through which each economy must pass as it grows. Early writers, given to metaphor, often stressed the resemblance between the evolutionary character of economic development and human life—e.g., growth, maturity, and decadence. Later writers, such as the Australian economist Colin Clark, have stressed the dominance of different sectors of an economy at different stages of its development and modernization. For Clark, development is a process of successive domination by primary (agriculture), secondary (manufacturing), and tertiary (trade and service) production. For the American economist W.W. Rostow, growth proceeds from a traditional society to a transitional one (in which the foundations for growth are developed), to the "take-off" society (in which development accelerates),

Entrepreneurs Sergey Brin and Larry Page, founders of Google. © AP Images

to the mature society. Various theories have been advanced to explain the movement from one stage to the next. Entrepreneurship and investment are the two factors most often singled out as critical.

Economic growth is usually distinguished from economic development, the latter term being restricted to economies that are close to the subsistence level. The term economic growth is applied to economies already experiencing rising per capita incomes. In Rostow's phraseology economic growth begins somewhere between the stage of take-off and the stage of maturity; or in Clark's terms, between the stage dominated by primary and the stage dominated by secondary production. The most striking aspect in such development is generally the enormous decrease in the proportion of the labour force employed in agriculture. There are other aspects of growth. The decline in agriculture and the rise of industry and services has led to concentration of the population in cities, first in what has come to be described as the "core city" and later in the suburbs. In earlier years public utility investment (including investment in transportation) was more important than manufacturing investment, but in the course of growth this relationship was reversed. There has also been a rise in the importance of durable consumer goods in total output. In the U.S. experience, the rate of growth of capital goods production at first exceeded the rate of growth of total output, but later this too was reversed. Likewise, business construction or plant expenditures loomed large in the earlier period as an object of business investment compared to the recent era. Whether other countries will go through the same experience at similar stages in their growth remains to be seen.

Comparative growth rates for a group of developed countries show how uneven the process of growth can be. Partly this unevenness reflects the extraordinary nature of the 1913–50 period, which included two major wars and a severe and prolonged depression. There are sizable differences, however, in the growth rates of the various countries as between the 1870–1913 and 1950–73 periods and the period since 1973. For the most part, these differences indicate an acceleration in rates of growth from the first to the second period and a marked slowdown in growth rates from the second to the current period. Many writers have attributed this to the more rapid growth of business investment during the middle of the three periods.

The relatively high rates of growth for West Germany, Japan, and Italy in the post-World War II period have stimulated a good deal of discussion. It is often argued that "late starters" can grow faster because they can borrow advanced technology from the early starters. In this way they leapfrog some of the stages of development that the early starters were forced to move through. This argument is nothing more than the assertion that late starters will grow rapidly during the period when they are modernizing. Italy did not succeed in growing rapidly and thereby modernizing until after World War II. Together with Japan and Germany it also experienced a large amount of war damage. This has an effect similar to starting late, since recovery from war entails building a stock of capital that will, other things being equal, embody the most advanced technology and therefore be more productive and allow faster growth. The other part of this argument is the assertion that early starters are actually deterred from introducing on a broad front the new technology they themselves have developed. For example, firms in a country that industrialized early may be inhibited from introducing a more modern and efficient means of transportation on a broad scale because there is no guarantee that other firms handling the ancillary loading and unloading tasks will also modernize to make the change profitable.

Related to this is the problem of whether or not per capita income levels and their rates of growth in developed economies will eventually converge or diverge. For example, as per capita incomes of fast growers like the Italians and Japanese approach those of economies that developed earlier, such as the American and British, will the growth rates of the former slow down? Economists who answer in the affirmative stress the similarities in the changing patterns of demand as per capita income rises. This emphasis in turn implies that there is less and less chance to borrow technology from the industrial leaders as the income levels of the late starters approach those of the more affluent. Moreover, rising per capita incomes in an affluent society usually are accompanied by a shift in demand toward services. Therefore, so this argument goes, differences in income levels and growth rates between countries should eventually narrow because of the low growth in productivity in the service sector. The evidence is inconclusive. On the one hand, growth is a function of something more than the ability to borrow the latest technology; on the other hand, it is not clear that productivity must always grow at a slower rate in the service industries.

A rapidly increasing population is not clearly either an advantage or a disadvantage to economic growth. The American Simon Kuznets and other investigators have found little association between rates of population growth and rates of growth of GNP per capita. Some of the fastest growing economies have been those with stable populations. And in the United States, where the rate of growth of population has shown a downward historical trend, the rate of growth of GNP per capita has increased over the last century and a half. Another finding by Kuznets is that while GNP per capita in 1960 was substantially higher in the United States than in any European country, there was no significant difference in the per capita growth rates of all these countries over the period

1840 to 1960 as a whole. The conclusion is that the United States started from a higher per capita base; this may have been the result of its superior natural resources, especially its fertile agricultural land.

While economic growth does not appear to be tied to population growth, it is a necessity to support a growing population—and the world's population is certainly growing. Therefore advocates of capitalism would argue that the spread of capitalism around the world has been an historical necessity because it creates the best opportunity for the global economy to create the jobs, incomes, and wealth to employ, shelter, and feed a fast-growing population.

Productivity Gains

Along with growth, productivity gains are another significant benefit of capitalism. Productivity, in economics, the ratio of what is produced to what is required to produce it. Usually this ratio is in the form of an average, expressing the total output of some category of goods divided by the total input of, say, labour or raw materials.

In principle, any input can be used in the denominator of the productivity ratio. Thus, one can speak of the productivity of land, labour, capital, or subcategories of any of these factors of production. One may also speak of the productivity of a certain type of fuel or raw material or may combine inputs to determine the productivity of labour and capital together or of all factors combined. The latter type of ratio is called "total factor" or "multifactor" productivity, and changes in it over time reflect the net saving of inputs per unit of output and thus increases in productive efficiency. It is sometimes also called the residual, since it reflects that portion of the growth of output that is not explained by increases in measured inputs. The partial productivity ratios of output to single inputs reflect not only changing productive efficiency but also the substitution of one factor for another—e.g., capital goods or energy for labour.

Labour is by far the most common of the factors used in measuring productivity. One reason for this is, of course, the relatively large share of labour costs in the value of most products. A second reason is that labour inputs are measured more easily than certain others, such as capital. This is especially true if by measurement one means simply counting heads and neglecting differences among workers in levels of skill and intensity of work. In addition, statistics of employment and labour-hours are often readily available, while information on other productive factors may be difficult to obtain. Although ratios of output to persons engaged in production or to labour-hours are referred to as labour productivity, the term does not imply that labour is solely responsible for changes in the ratio. Improvements in output per unit of labour may be due to increased quality and efficiency of the human factor but also to many other variables discussed later. There is special interest in labour productivity measures, however, since human beings are the end as well as a means of production.

The significance of productivity is that a nation or an industry advances by using less to make more. Labour productivity is an especially sensitive indicator of this economizing process and is one of the major measures used to chart a nation's or an industry's economic advance. An overall rise in a nation's labour productivity signifies the potential availability of a larger quantity of goods and services per worker than before and, accordingly, a potential for higher real income per worker. Countries with high real wages are usually also those with high labour productivity, while those with low real wages are generally low in productivity. If, for the moment, other productive factors are neglected, one can see that the wage level will then be equal to the total national product divided by the number of workers; that is, it will be equal to the level of labour productivity.

Real average labour compensation has increased over the long run at about the same pace as labour productivity. The association of these two variables must be close so long as the labour share of total cost does not change much. If nominal average earnings were to increase more than labour productivity, labour cost per unit of output would rise and so would prices unless profit margins were reduced to compensate. In general, prices rise by less than wage rates and other input prices to the extent that total productivity rises. Productivity growth is thus an anti-inflationary factor, although inflation is basically a monetary phenomenon.

There is a significant negative correlation between relative industry changes in productivity and in prices—when productivity rises, price tends to fall. In the industrial sector of an economy in which there is a significant price elasticity of demand (i.e., where price is relatively responsive to changes in demand), there is also a significant positive correlation between relative industry changes in productivity and in output—when productivity rises, output tends to rise as well. This is an interactive relationship, since the tendency of price to fall as productivity increases is reinforced by the tendency of economies of scale made possible by increased output to further enhance productivity.

In dynamic economies the supply of capital has risen faster than the size of the labour force, and wage rates have risen faster than the price of capital. As a result there has been a marked tendency to substitute capital for labour in almost all industries. Yet there has been no long-term trend toward increased unemployment because real aggregate demand has tended to rise enough to absorb the growth of the labour force. Cyclical fluctuations in output and employment in capitalist countries are not the result of technological displacements of labour but rather reflect macroeconomic variables, such as growth of the money supply, that affect aggregate demand.

Productivity, then, contributes to the growth of wages, the growth of jobs, and keeping prices under control. Capitalism creates economic incentives for companies to pursue productivity gains, and so a capitalist system can also be seen as a route to more jobs, higher wages, and lower prices.

Criticisms of Capitalism

Unfortunately, capitalism does not always work as well in practice as it does in theory. There have been times when the system has failed to deliver growth overall, and capitalism almost always leaves some segments of the population behind. The following are some common criticisms of capitalism.

The Unreliability of Growth

The first of these problems is already familiar from the previous discussion of the stages of capitalist development. Many critics have alleged that the capitalist system suffers from inherent instability that has characterized and plagued the system since the advent of industrialization. Because capitalist growth is driven by profit expectations, it fluctuates with the changes in technological or social opportunities for capital accumulation. As opportunities appear, capital rushes in to take advantage of them, bringing as a consequence the familiar attributes of a boom. Sooner or later, however, the rush subsides as the demand for the new products or services becomes saturated, bringing a halt to investment, a shakeout in the main industries caught up in the previous boom, and the advent of recession. Hence, economic growth comes at the price of a succession of market gluts as booms meet their inevitable end.

This criticism did not receive its full exposition until the publication of the first volume of Marx's *Das Kapital* in 1867. For Marx, the path of growth is not only unstable for the reasons just mentioned—Marx called such uncoordinated movements the "anarchy" of the market—but increasingly unstable. Marx believed that the reason for this is also familiar. It is the result of the industrialization process, which leads toward large-scale enterprises. As each saturation brings growth to a halt, a process of winnowing takes place in which the more successful firms are able to acquire the assets of the less successful. Thus, the very dynamics of growth tend to concentrate capital into ever-larger firms. This leads to still more massive disruptions when the next boom ends, a process that terminates, according to Marx, only when the temper of the working class snaps and capitalism is replaced by socialism.

Beginning in the 1930s, Marx's apocalyptic expectations were largely replaced by the less-violent but equally disquieting views of the English economist John Maynard Keynes, first set forth in his influential *The General Theory of Employment, Interest, and Money* (1936). Keynes believed that the basic problem of capitalism is not so much its vulnerability to periodic saturations of investment as its likely failure to recover from them. He raised the possibility that a capitalist system could remain indefinitely in a condition of equilibrium despite high unemployment, a possibility not only entirely novel (even Marx believed that the system would recover its momentum after each crisis) but also made plausible by the persistent unemployment of the 1930s. Keynes therefore raised the prospect that growth would end in stagnation, a condition for which the only remedy he saw was "a somewhat comprehensive socialization of investment."

The Quality of Growth

A second criticism with respect to market-driven growth focuses on the adverse side effects generated by a system of production that is held accountable only to the test of profitability. It is in the nature of a complex industrial society that the production processes of many commodities generate "bads" as well as "goods"—e.g., toxic wastes or unhealthy working conditions as well as useful products.

The catalog of such market-generated ills is very long. Smith himself warned that the division of labour, by routinizing work, would render workers "as stupid and ignorant as it is possible for a human creature to become," and Marx raised the spectre of alienation as the social price paid for subordinating production to the imperatives of profit making. Other economists warned that the introduction of technology designed to cut labour costs would create permanent unemployment. In modern times much attention has focused on the power of physical and chemical processes to surpass the carrying capacity of the environment—a concern made cogent by various types of environmental damage arising from excessive discharges of industrial effluents and pollutants. Because these social and ecological challenges spring from the extraordinary powers of technology, they can be viewed as side effects of socialist as well as capitalist growth. But the argument can be made that market growth, by virtue of its overriding obedience to profit, is congenitally blind to such externalities.

Equity

A third criticism of capitalist growth concerns the fairness with which capitalism distributes its expanding wealth or with which it shares its recurrent hardships. This criticism assumes both specific and general forms.

One criticism of capitalism is that it creates a wide disparity in income.
Bloomberg/Getty Images

The specific form focuses on disparities in income among layers of the population. At the turn of the 21st century in the United States, for example, the lowest fifth of all households received only 3.6 percent of total income, whereas the topmost fifth received 49 percent. Significantly, this disparity results from the concentration of assets in the upper brackets. Also, the disparity is the consequence of highly skewed patterns of corporate rewards that typically give, say, chief executive officers of large companies 50 to 100 times more income than those of ordinary office or factory employees. Income disparities, however, should be understood in perspective, as they stem from a number of causes. In its 1995 annual report the Federal Reserve Bank of Dallas observed,

> By definition, there will always be a bottom 20 percent, but only in a strict caste society will it contain the same individuals and families year after year.

Moving from specific examples of distribution to a more general level, the criticism may be broadened to an indictment of the market principle itself as the regulator of incomes. An advocate of market-determined distribution will declare that in a market-based society, with certain exceptions, people tend to be paid what they are worth—that is, their incomes will reflect the value of their contribution to production. Thus, market-based rewards lead to the efficiency of the productive system and thereby maximize the total income available for distribution. This argument is countered at two levels. Marxist critics contend that labourers in a capitalist economy are systematically paid less than the value of their work by virtue of the superior bargaining power of employers, so that the claim of efficiency masks an underlying condition of exploitation. Other critics question the criterion of efficiency itself, which counts every dollar of input and output but pays no heed to the moral or social or aesthetic qualities of either and which excludes workers from expressing their own preferences as to the most appropriate decisions for their firms.

Corrective Measures

Various measures have been taken by capitalist societies to meet these criticisms, although it must be recognized that a deep disagreement divides economists with respect to the accuracy of the criticisms, let alone the appropriate corrective measures to be adopted if these criticisms are valid. A substantial body of economists believe that many of the difficulties of the system spring not from its own workings but from well-meaning attempts to block or channel them. Thus, with respect to the problem of instability, supporters of the market system believe that capitalism, left alone as much as possible, will naturally corroborate the trend of economic expansion that has marked its history. They also expect that whatever instabilities appear tend quickly to correct themselves, provided that government plays a generally passive role. Market-oriented economists do not deny that the system can give rise to qualitative or distributional ills, but they tend to believe that these are more than compensated for by its general expansive properties. Where specific problems remain, such as damage to the environment or serious poverty, the prescription often seeks to utilize the market system itself as the corrective agency—e.g., alleviating poverty through negative income taxes rather than with welfare payments or controlling pollution by charging fees on the outflow of wastes rather than by banning the discharge of pollutants.

Opposing this view is a much more interventionist approach rooted in generally Keynesian and welfare-oriented policies. This view doubts the intrinsic momentum or reliability of capitalist growth and is therefore prepared to use active government means, both fiscal and monetary, to combat recession. It is also more sceptical of the likelihood of improving the quality or the equity of society by market means and, although not opposing these, looks more favourably on direct regulatory intervention and on specific programs of assistance to disprivileged groups.

Despite this philosophical division of opinion, a fair degree of practical consensus was reached on a number of issues in the 1950s and '60s. Although there are differences in policy style and determination from one nation to the next, all capitalist governments have taken measures to overcome recession—whether by lowering taxes, by borrowing and spending, or by easing interest rates—and all pursue the opposite kinds of policies in inflationary times. It cannot be said that these policies have been unqualified successes, either in bringing about vigorous or steady growth or in ridding the system of its inflationary tendencies. Yet, imperfect though they are, these measures seem to have been sufficient to prevent the development of socially destructive depressions on the order of the Great Depression of the 1930s. It is not the eradication but the limitation of instability that has been a signal achievement of all advanced capitalist countries since World War II. It should be noted, however, that these remedial measures have little or no international application. Although the World Bank and the International Monetary Fund make efforts on behalf of developing countries, no institution exists to control credit for the world (as do the central banks that control it for individual nations); no global spending or taxing authority can speed up, or hold back, the pace of production for industrial regions as a whole; no agency effectively oversees the availability of credit for the developing nations or the feasibility of the terms on which it may be extended. Thus, some critics of globalization contend that the internationalization of capitalism may exert destabilizing influences for which no policy corrective as yet exists.

A broadly similar appraisal can be made with respect to the redress of specific threats that emerge as unintended consequences of the market system. The issue is largely one of scale. Specific problems can often be redressed by market incentives to alter behaviour (paying a fee for returning used bottles) or, when the effect is more serious, by outright prohibition (bans on child labour or on dangerous chemical fertilizers). The problem becomes less amenable to control, however, when the market generates unintended consequences of large proportions, such as traffic congestion in cities. The difficulty here is that the correction of such externalities requires the support and cooperation of the public and thereby crosses the line from the economic into the political arena, often making redress more difficult to obtain. On a still larger scale, the remedy for some problems may require international agreements, and these often raise conflicts of interest between the nation generating the ill effects as a by-product of its own production and those suffering from the effects. The problem of acid rain originating in one country but falling in another is a case in point. Again the economic problem becomes political and its control more complicated.

A number of remedies have been applied to the distributional problems of capitalism. No advanced capitalist country today allows the market to distribute income without supplementing or altering the resulting pattern of rewards through taxes, subsidies, welfare systems, or entitlement payments such as old-age pensions and health benefits. In the United States, these transfer payments, as they are called, amount to some 10 percent of total consumer income; in a number of European nations, they come to considerably more. The result has been to lessen considerably the incidence of officially measured poverty.

Yet these examples of successful corrective action by governments do not go unchallenged by economists who are concerned that some of the "cures" applied to social problems may be worse than the "disease." While admitting that the market system fails to live up to its ideal, these economists argue that government correctives and collective decision making must be subjected to the same critical scrutiny leveled against the market system. Markets may fail, in other words, but so might governments. The stagflation of the 1970s, the fiscal crises of some democratic states in the 1980s, and the double-digit unemployment in western Europe in the 1990s set the stage for the 21st century by raising serious doubts about the ability of government correctives to solve market problems. Even so, the global financial crisis in 2008 also raised serious doubts about the market's ability to solve its own problems.

A Real-life Tug of War: The Robber Barons and the Trust Busters

As noted in the previous section of this chapter, even within capitalist systems there is an ongoing debate over the ability of government to address some of the difficulties that come with the exercise of capitalism. One of the early and most prominent conflicts to arise from this debate was the early 20th-century confrontation between America's so-called robber barons and trust busters.

During the latter half of the 19th century, control of much of the industrial production of the United States was consolidated in the hands of a small group of business tycoons commonly referred to as the "robber barons." The nickname related to criticisms of their business practices, which often involved using their power to dominate workers, control prices, and stifle competition.

For example, John D. Rockefeller's Standard Oil Company gained control of 90 to 95 percent of all oil produced in the United States by 1880. It did this through elimination of competitors, mergers with other firms, and use of favourable railroad rebates.

Robber Barons

John D. Rockefeller was one of a group of powerful, late 19th century American businessmen frequently referred to as "robber barons." Others included J.P. Morgan, Andrew Carnegie, and Andrew Mellon. Perhaps the most notorious, though, was a financier named Jay Gould.

Gould had a long history of investing in railroad companies when, in 1868, he joined Daniel Drew and Jim Fisk in a struggle to keep Cornelius Vanderbilt from wresting away their control of the Erie railroad. To this end, Gould engaged in outrageous financial manipulations, including the issue of fraudulent stock and the payment of lavish bribes to New York state legislators to legalize that stock's sale. Gould ended up in control of the railroad, and he and Fisk then joined forces with William "Boss" Tweed and Peter Sweeney to profit from further unscrupulous speculations using Erie stock. The four men's attempt to corner the market in loose gold caused the panic of "Black Friday" (Sept. 24, 1869), when the price, in paper money, of $100 in gold specie, after being driven up to $163.50 by market bidding, fell to $133 when the U.S. Treasury placed $4 million in specie on the market. The disastrous panic that ensued ruined many investors and led to a public outcry against Gould, who was finally forced to relinquish control of the Erie Railroad in 1872, after Fisk had died and the Tweed Ring in New York City had been broken up.

Now possessed of a fortune of $25 million, Gould turned his attention to railroads in the West. He began buying large blocks of Union Pacific Railroad stock and acquired control of that railway by 1874. He bought other lines as well, so that by 1881, at its peak, his railroad empire was the largest one in the nation, totalling about 15,800 miles (25,500 km) of track, or 15 percent of the United States' total rail mileage. Having made large profits from manipulating the company's stock, Gould pulled out of the Union Pacific by 1882. He began building a new railway system, centred on the Missouri Pacific Railroad, that constituted one-half of all trackage in the Southwest by 1890.

In 1881 Gould gained control of the Western Union Telegraph Company after he had weakened that company with cutthroat competition from his own smaller telegraph companies. Gould also owned the *New York World* newspaper from 1879 to 1883, and by 1886 he had acquired the Manhattan Elevated Railroad, which held a monopoly over New York City's elevated railways. Gould remained ruthless, unscrupulous,

(continued on the next page)

and friendless to the end and died leaving a fortune estimated at $77 million.

Not all of the robber barons' tactics were as unscrupulous as Gould's, and many are respected by history as important businessmen and philanthropists. However, what they had in common with Gould was a certain ruthlessness in the pursuit of massive wealth – a trait which still can lead to both great riches and public disfavour.

In 1882 the Standard Oil Company and affiliated companies that were engaged in producing, refining, and marketing oil were combined in the Standard Oil Trust, created by the Standard Oil Trust Agreement signed by nine trustees, including Rockefeller. By the agreement, companies could be purchased, created, dissolved, merged, or divided; eventually, the trustees governed some 40 corporations, of which 14 were wholly owned. Founded in 1882, Standard Oil of New Jersey was one component of the trust; by design the Standard Oil Trust embraced a maze of legal structures, which made its workings virtually impervious to public investigation and understanding. As Ida Tarbell wrote in her *History of the Standard Oil Company* (1904), "You could argue its existence from its effects, but you could not prove it." In 1892 the Ohio Supreme Court ordered the trust dissolved, but it effectively continued to operate from headquarters in New York City.

In 1899, however, the company renamed its New Jersey firm Standard Oil Company (New Jersey) and incorporated it as a holding company. All assets and interests formerly grouped in the trust were transferred to the New Jersey company, representing a further concentration of industry control.

Although consolidation did advance the large-scale production and distribution of oil products, many critics believed that the resulting concentration of economic power was becoming excessive. In 1906 the U.S. government brought suit against Standard Oil Company (New Jersey) under the Sherman Antitrust Act of 1890; in 1911 the New Jersey company was ordered to divest itself of its major holdings—33 companies in all. This decentralization made it impossible for Standard Oil to exert its former control over the petroleum industry in the United States.

The Sherman Act had been the first legislation enacted by the United States Congress (1890) to curb concentrations of power that interfere with trade and reduce economic competition. It was named for U.S. Senator John Sherman of Ohio, who was an expert on the regulation of commerce.

Antitrust cartoon (1889) depicting giant corporations as the rulers of the Senate. Private Collection/Peter Newark American Pictures/The Bridgeman Art Library

One of the act's main provisions outlaws all combinations that restrain trade between states or with foreign nations. This prohibition applies not only to formal cartels but also to any agreement to fix prices, limit industrial output, share markets, or exclude competition. A second key provision makes illegal all attempts to monopolize any part of trade or commerce in the United States. These two provisions, which comprise the heart of the Sherman Act, are enforceable by the Department of Justice through litigation in the federal courts. Firms found in violation of the act can be ordered dissolved by the courts, and injunctions to prohibit illegal practices can be issued. Violations are punishable by fines and imprisonment. Moreover, private parties injured by violations are permitted to sue for triple the amount of damages done them.

For more than a decade after its passage, the Sherman Act was invoked only rarely against industrial monopolies, and then not successfully, chiefly because of narrow judicial interpretations of what constitutes trade or commerce among states. Its only effective use was against trade unions, which were held by the courts to be illegal combinations. The first vigorous enforcement of the Sherman Act occurred during the administration of President Theodore Roosevelt (1901–09). In 1914 Congress passed two legislative measures that provided support for the Sherman Act. One of these was the Clayton Antitrust Act, which elaborated on the general provisions of the Sherman Act and specified many illegal practices that either contributed to or resulted from monopolization. The other measure created the Federal Trade Commission (FTC), providing the government with an agency that had the power to investigate possible violations of antitrust legislation and issue orders forbidding unfair competition practices.

The Sherman Act, and in particular the vigorous use of it by Theodore Roosevelt and others who followed him, represented a significant milestone in the tug of war between free market advocates and those who felt it was government's role to promote fairness in how capitalism was pursued in the United States. Roosevelt and his allies, known collectively as the "trust busters" for their efforts to curb far-reaching organizations like the Standard Oil Trust, showed that the government was willing to exert some control over the market – particularly in response to narrow interests that were trying to control the market themselves.

CONCLUSION

As complicated as capitalism can seem, it is also the stuff of everyday, ordinary life. Every time people buy groceries, collect a paycheck, or make an investment, they are actively participating in capitalism.

This everyday aspect of capitalism may be the biggest reason why learning about how it operates is so important. Abstract concepts of supply and demand turn into flesh and blood reality when people work to provide a product or service, or when they make decisions as consumers.

Decisions, after all, are what capitalism is all about. Adam Smith wrote about people making decisions based on their incentives and self-interest, and decision-making permeates the history and study of capitalism.

So, for people who have no interest in making the study of economics a long-term pursuit, the concepts introduced in this book should at least help provide the understanding necessary to make better financial, career, and consumer decisions. After all, decisions such as whether to lease or buy a car, whether to take a certain job, or whether to buy a new product now or later are all impacted by the principles of capitalism introduced in this book.

Other people may want to go further than everyday applications of capitalism, and pursue a detailed study of it. For some, the complexity is an inspiring challenge; for others, the lure might be that the lingering mysteries about how capitalism works present a puzzle to be solved. Still others may feel passionately about some of the viewpoints in the capitalist debate, and seek the knowledge to help promote one of those viewpoints.

After all, whether one believes in the primacy of free markets, the responsibility of government to regulate those markets, or the application of market forces to help society, there are arguments to be found in the study of capitalism. Studying the history and concepts in this book can provide a person with the material to participate in those debates, and perhaps help advance them.

GLOSSARY

assembly line Industrial arrangement of machines, equipment, and workers for continuous flow of workpieces in mass-production operations.

bourgeois Relating to or belonging to the middle class of society.

business cycle Periodic fluctuations in the general rate of economic activity, as measured by the levels of employment, prices, and production.

capital A stock of resources that may be employed in the production of goods and services.

capitalism An economic system characterized by private or corporate ownership of capital goods, by investments that are determined by private decision, and by prices, production, and the distribution of goods that are determined mainly by competition in a free market.

capitalist A person who has uses money and property to produce more money, or a person who believes that capitalism is the best kind of economic system.

capital markets The part of a financial system concerned with raising capital by dealing in shares, bonds, and other long-term investments.

cartel Association of independent firms or individuals for the purpose of exerting some form of restrictive or monopolistic influence on the production or sale of a commodity.

command economy Economic system in which the means of production are publicly owned and economic activity is controlled by a central authority that assigns quantitative production goals and allots raw materials to productive enterprises.

competition Rivalry among many buyers and sellers, with opportunity for new companies to enter the market.

consumer A person who buys goods and services.

corporatism The organization of a society into industrial and professional corporations serving as organs of political representation and exercising control over persons and activities within their jurisdiction.

currency Money, such as coins, treasury notes, and banknotes, that is in circulation as a medium of exchange.

demand Willingness and ability to purchase a commodity or service.

depression Major downswing in the business cycle that is characterized by sharply reduced industrial production, widespread unemployment, serious declines or cessations of growth in construction activity, and great reductions in international trade and capital movements.

distribution channel Way of marketing or selling a company's product either directly or through distributors, such as wholesalers, small retailers, retail chains, or direct mailers.

division of labour The separation of a work process into a number of tasks, with each task performed by a separate person or group of persons.

entrepreneur A person who starts a business and is willing to risk loss in order to make money.

federal reserve The central banking system of the United States consisting of 12 districts with a Federal Reserve bank in the principal commercial city of each district.

fiscal policy Measures employed by governments to stabilize the economy, specifically by manipulating the levels and allocations of taxes and government expenditures.

globalization Development of an increasingly integrated global economy marked especially by free trade, free flow of capital, and the tapping of cheaper foreign labor markets.

gold standard Monetary standard under which the basic unit of currency is defined by a stated quantity of gold and which is usually characterized by the coinage and circulation of gold, unrestricted convertibility of other money into gold, and the free export and import of gold for settling of international obligations.

industrialization The process of converting to a socioeconomic order in which industry is dominant.

innovation The introduction of something new.

intellectual property Property, such as an idea, invention, or process, that derives from the work of the mind or intellect.

interest The price paid for the use of credit or money.

Keynesian economics Body of ideas set forth by John Maynard Keynes in his *General Theory of Employment, Interest and Money* (1935–36) and other works, intended to provide a theoretical basis for government full-employment policies.

manufacturing Any industry that makes products from raw materials by the use of manual labour or machinery and that is usually carried out systematically with a division of labour.

market cycle Times of economic expansion and prosperity followed by economic downturns.

mass production Application of the principles of specialization, division of labour, and standardization of parts to the manufacture of goods.

means of production The materials and resources used to produce goods.

monetary policy Measures employed by governments to influence economic activity, specifically by manipulating the supplies of money and credit and by altering rates of interest.

money supply The liquid assets held by individuals and banks.

monopoly An exclusive possession of a market by a supplier of a product or a service for which there is no substitute.

organized labour Association and activities of workers in a trade or industry for the purpose of obtaining or assuring improvements in working conditions through their collective action.

personal freedom Freedom of the person in going and coming, equality before the courts, security of private property, freedom of opinion and its expression, and freedom of conscience subject to the rights of others and of the public.

property rights A legal right or interest in or against specific property.

recession A downward trend in the business cycle characterized by a decline in production and employment, which in turn causes the incomes and spending of households to decline.

standard of living A measure of the consumption of goods and services by an individual or group.

supply The amount of something that is available to be used.

trust Arrangement in which someone's property or money is legally held or managed by someone else or by an organization (such as a bank) for usually a set period of time.

unemployment The total number of people who do not have jobs in a particular place or area.

World Trade Organization International organization established to supervise and liberalize world trade.

BIBLIOGRAPHY

General texts

Historical analysis is presented in Robert L. Heilbroner, *The Making of Economic Society*, 11th ed. (2002). An excellent presentation along more functional lines, well-written but requiring some acquaintance with economic theory, is Frederic L. Pryor, *A Guidebook to the Comparative Study of Economic Systems* (1985). Morris Bornstein (ed.), *Comparative Economic Systems: Models and Cases*, 7th ed. (1994), a book of readings, is also recommended.

Capitalism

Two broad treatments of capitalism are Adam Smith, *An Inquiry into the Nature and Causes of the Wealth of Nations* (1776); and Karl Marx, *Das Kapital*, vol. 1, trans. by Samuel Moore and Edward Aveling as *Capital: A Critical Analysis of Capitalist Production* (1886); both works are available in many later editions. Robert L. Heilbroner, *The Nature and Logic of Capitalism* (1985), treats the social formation of capitalism. Fernand Braudel, *Civilization and Capitalism, 15th–18th Century*, 3 vol. (1982–84, reissued 1992; originally published in French, 1979), is a wide-ranging overview. Nathan Rosenberg and L.E. Birdzell, Jr., *How the West Grew Rich: The Economic Transformation of the Industrial World* (1986, reissued 1999), discusses the Industrial Revolution and the rise of capitalism. John Kenneth Galbraith, *The New Industrial State*, 4th ed. (1985), is a modern classic. Milton Friedman, *Capitalism and Freedom* (1962, reissued 2002); and Milton Friedman and

Rose Friedman, *Free to Choose* (1980, reissued 1990), are perhaps the most accessible treatments of economics and public policy from a market-oriented perspective.

Markets

Glenn G. Munn, F.L. Garcia, and Charles J. Woelfel, *Encyclopedia of Banking and Finance*, 9th ed., rev. and expanded (also published as *The St. James Encyclopedia of Banking & Finance*, 1991), provides comprehensive definitions, many with bibliographies. Edward I. Altman and Mary Jane McKinney (eds.), *Handbook of Financial Markets and Institutions*, 6th ed. (1987), is a thorough compilation. Detailed information on a variety of markets is provided in Francis A. Lees and Maximo Eng, *International Financial Markets: Development of the Present System and Future Prospects* (1975), a descriptive treatment; Charles R. Geisst, *A Guide to the Financial Markets*, 2nd ed. (1989), for the general reader; Frank J. Fabozzi and Frank G. Zarb, *Handbook of Financial Markets: Securities, Options, and Futures*, 2nd ed. (1986); and Perry J. Kaufman, *Handbook of Futures Markets: Commodity, Financial, Stock Index, and Options* (1984), including the history, regulation, and mechanics of futures trading. Further discussion of financial futures is found in Mark J. Powers and Mark G. Castelino, *Inside the Financial Futures Markets*, 3rd ed. (1991), an explanation of the exchanges and their functions; and Nancy H. Rothstein and James M. Little (eds.), *The Handbook of Financial Futures: A Guide for Investors and Professional Financial Managers* (1984), a discussion of the market's development, organization, and regulation.

The first chapter of Adam Smith, *An Inquiry into the Nature and Causes of the Wealth of Nations* (1776, reprinted frequently), contains his famous discussion of the division of labour. Alfred Marshall, *Principles of Economics*, 9th ed., 2 vol. (1961), conveys his approach to the market. The development of the general equilibrium approach to markets by Leon Walrus and others is well recounted by Joseph A. Schumpeter, *A History of Economic Analysis*, ed. by Elizabeth Boody Schumpeter (1954). The best short introduction to the Keynesian Revolution is by Michal Kalecki, *Studies in the Theory of Business Cycles, 1933–1939* (1966; originally published in Polish, 1962). These essays were written before the publication of the great work of John Maynard Keynes, *The General Theory of Employment, Interest, and Money* (1935, reissued 1991). A critical account of the theory of imperfect competition is presented in the preface to Joan Robinson, *The Economics of Imperfect Competition*, 2nd ed. (1969, reissued 1976). A slightly different approach is that of Edward Hastings Chamberlin, *The Theory of Monopolistic Competition*, 8th ed. (1962). Economies without markets are described in Karl Polanyi, *Primitive, Archaic, and Modern Economies*, ed. by George Dalton (1968), a collection of essays of great interest and originality. Andrew Shonfield, *Modern Capitalism* (1965, reissued 1978), studies the ways in which various countries have adapted their economic administration to modern requirements. A more critical view of modern capitalism is that of John Kenneth Galbraith, *The New Industrial State*, 4th ed. (1985). A Marxist view is set forth by Paul Baran and Paul Sweezy, *Monopoly Capital* (1966). A summary of the attempts at economic reform in the then-existent Soviet Union and other countries with socialist economies is given in Michael Ellman, *Economic Reform in the Soviet Union* (1969). The economic problems of the poor countries are examined in Gunnar Myrdal, The Challenge of World Poverty (1970), a continuation of his monumental work *Asian Drama: An Inquiry into the Poverty of Nations*, 3 vol. (1968), also available in an abridged edition (1971).

The classic appraisal of the market from the standpoint of social welfare is A.C. Pigou, *The Economics of Welfare*, 4th ed. (1962). Appraisals of welfare economics include I.M.D. Little, *A Critique of Welfare Economics*, 2nd ed. (1957, reissued 1970); J. de V. Graaff, *Theoretical Welfare Economics* (1957, reissued 1975); and Maurice Dobb, *On Economic Theory and Socialism* (1955, reissued 1972). Thorstein Veblen, *The Place of Science in Modern Civilisation, and Other Essays* (1919, reprinted 1990), most directly expresses his critique of the market ideology.

Adam Smith

The complete works of Adam Smith have appeared in a definitive edition, The *Glasgow Edition of the Works and Correspondence of Adam Smith*, 6 vol. in 7 (1976–83), including vol. 1, *The Theory of Moral Sentiments*, ed. by D.D. Raphael and A.L. MacFie (1976, reprinted 1984); vol. 2, *An Inquiry into the Nature and Causes of the Wealth of Nations*, ed. by R.H. Campbell and A.S. Skinner, 2 vol. (1976, reprinted 1981); vol. 3, *Essays on Philosophical Subjects*, ed. by W.P.D. Wightman and J.C. Bryce (1980, reprinted 1982), which contains the interesting "The History of Astronomy"; vol. 4, *Lectures on Rhetoric and Belles Lettres*, ed. by J.C. Bryce (1983, reprinted 1985); and vol. 5, *Lectures on Jurisprudence*, ed. by R.L. Meek, D.D. Raphael, and P.G. Stein (1978, reprinted 1982). For the nonspecialist, Robert L. Heilbroner (ed.), *The Essential Adam Smith* (1986), offers fairly extensive readings and short discussions of Smith's main works.

Among biographical works are Ian Simpson Ross, *The Life of Adam Smith* (1995); John Rae, *Life of Adam Smith* (1895, reprinted 1990); William R. Scott, *Adam Smith as Student and Professor* (1937, reprinted 1965), containing various documents and correspondence, including "An Early Draft of Part of *The Wealth of Nations*"; and Dugald Stewart, *Biographical Memoirs of Adam Smith*..., vol. 10 (1811), in The Collected Works of Dugald Stewart (1854–60, reprinted 1994).

Donald Winch, Adam Smith's Politics: An Essay in Historiographic Revision (1978), reinterprets Smith's place in the history of economic and political thought; while Emma Rothschild, Economic Sentiments: Adam Smith, Condorcet, and the Enlightenment (2001), reconsiders the nature of Enlightenment thinking. Andrew S. Skinner and Thomas Wilson, Essays on Adam Smith (1975), contains discussion by well-known scholars of various aspects of Smith's work. Knud Haakonssen, *The Science of a Legislator: The Natural Jurisprudence of David Hume and Adam Smith* (1981), compares their philosophical systems.

Useful articles include Adolph Lowe, "The Classical Theory of Economic Growth," *Social Research*, 21(2):127–158 (Summer 1954); Nathan Rosenberg, "Adam Smith on the Division of Labour: Two Views or One?," *Economica*, 32(126):127–139 (May 1965), and "Some Institutional Aspects of *The Wealth of Nations*," *The Journal of Political Economy*, 68(6):557–570 (December 1960); and Joseph J. Spengler, "Adam Smith's Theory of Economic Growth," *Southern Economic Journal*, 25(4):397–415, 26(1):1–12 (April and July 1959).

Monopoly and Competition

Noteworthy texts include William Fellner, *Competition Among the Few: Oligopoly and Similar Market Structures* (1949, reissued 1965), a highly sophisticated and stimulating development of the theory of oligopoly; Joe S. Bain, *Barriers to New Competition: Their Character and Consequences in Manufacturing Industries*

(1956, reissued 1993), a thorough introduction to the notion of barriers to entry, and *Industrial Organization*, 2nd ed. (1968, reissued 1987), a general textbook covering theoretical and empirical aspects of problems of monopoly and competition; Carl Kaysen and Donald F. Turner, *Antitrust Policy: An Economic and Legal Analysis* (1959, reissued 1965), a superior analysis and criticism of the working of American antitrust policies; Edward Chamberlin, *Theory of Monopolistic Competition*, 8th ed. (1962, reissued 1969), a classic and germinal contribution to the theory of markets; Joan Robinson, *Economics of Imperfect Competition*, 2nd ed. (1969, reissued 1976), a penetrating theoretical analysis of monopolistic and quasi-monopolistic pricing; and William G. Shepherd and Clair Wilcox, *Public Policies Toward Business*, 8th ed. (1991), a good general textbook including extensive treatment of policies affecting monopoly and competition.

Joseph A. Schumpeter, *Capitalism, Socialism, and Democracy*, 6th ed. (1987), provides an enduringly brilliant analysis of various market structures. Charles E. Lindblom, *Politics and Markets: The World's Political Economic Systems* (1977), is another classic that provides an excellent examination of market structures; and Richard E. Quandt and Dusan Triska (eds.), *Optimal Decisions in Markets and Planned Economies* (1990), examines themes treated by Lindblom. Special topics related to market structure can be found in Don E. Waldman, *Antitrust Action and Market Structure* (1978); and Elhanan Helpman and Paul R. Krugman, *Trade Policy and Market Structure* (1989).

Excellent treatments of industrial organization include Jean Tirole, *The Theory of Industrial Organization* (1988), a graduate-level text; Richard Schmalensee and Robert D. Willig (eds.), *Handbook of Industrial Organization*, 5th ed., 2 vol. (1998), a reference book at the graduate level; and Dennis W. Carlton and Jeffrey M. Perloff, *Modern Industrial Organization*, 4th ed. (2005), an accessible intermediate-level text.

Price System

The classic work on the history of economic theory, particularly of value theory, is Joseph Schumpeter, *History of Economic Analysis*, ed. by Elizabeth Boody Schumpeter (1954, reissued 1986). Pioneering works on the informational role of the price system are presented in F.A. Hayek, *Individualism and Economic Order* (1948), in particular the essays "The Use of Knowledge in Society" and "Economics and Knowledge." An excellent brief discussion can be found in George J. Stigler, *Essays in the History of Economics* (1965, reprinted 1987), especially essays 5, 6, and 12. Advanced works on modern value theory are J.R. Hicks, Value and Capital, 2nd ed. (1950, reissued 1974); and Paul A. Samuelson, *Foundations of Economic Analysis*, enlarged ed. (1983).

Major historical treatises include Adam Smith, *An Inquiry into the Nature and Causes of the Wealth of Nations*, 2 vol. (1776, reissued in 1 vol., 1991); and John Stuart Mill, *Principles of Political Economy*, 2 vol. (1848, reissued in 1 vol., 1994). Selected applied analyses include R.A. Radford, "The Economic Organization of a P.O.W. Camp," *Economica*, 12:189–201 (1945), an account of the evolution of a cigarette-based price system; and Reuben A. Kessel, R.H. Coase, and Merton H. Miller (eds.), *Essays in Applied Price Theory* (1980).

Seminal works in the history of value theory include David Ricardo, *On the Principles of Political Economy and Taxation* (1817, reissued 1981); F.Y. Edgeworth, *Mathematical Psychics* (1881, reprinted 1967); Vilfredo Pareto, *Cours d'économie politique*,

2 vol. (1896–97); J.R. Hicks and R.D.G. Allen, "A Reconsideration of the Theory of Value," *Economica*, New Series, 2 parts, 1:52–76,196–219 (1934); R.G.D. Allen, "Professor Slutsky's Theory of Consumers' Choice," *The Review of Economic Studies*, 3:120–129 (1936); Carl Menger, *Principles of Economics* (1950, reissued 1981; originally published in German, 1871); Léon Walras, *Elements of Pure Economics; or, The Theory of Social Wealth* (1954, reprinted 1984; originally published in French, 1874); W. Stanley Jevons, *The Theory of Political Economy*, 5th ed. (1957); and Alfred Marshall, *Principles of Economics*, 9th ed., 2 vol. (1961), also discussing price.

Money

Works on various aspects of monetary history include Phillip Cagan, "The Monetary Dynamics of Hyperinflation," in Milton Friedman (ed.), *Studies in the Quantity Theory of Money* (1956, reissued 1973); Paul Einzig, *Primitive Money in Its Ethnological, Historical, and Economic Aspects*, 2nd ed. rev. (1966); Albert E. Feavearyear, *The Pound Sterling: A History of English Money*, 2nd ed. (1963); Milton Friedman and Anna Jacobson Schwartz, *A Monetary History of the United States, 1867–1960* (1963, reissued 1993), and *Monetary Trends in the United States and the United Kingdom* (1982); and Allan H. Meltzer, *A History of the Federal Reserve*, 1 vol. (2002–).

Useful readings in monetary theory, of varying levels of difficulty, include John Maynard Keynes, *A Treatise on Money*, 2 vol. (1930, reprinted 1976); Don Patinkin, *Money, Interest, and Prices: An Integration of Monetary and Value Theory*, 2nd ed. (1989); Dennis Holme Robertson, *Money*, new ed. (1959, reissued 1966); Karl Brunner and Allan H. Meltzer, *Money and the Economy: Issues in Monetary Analysis* (1993, reissued 1997); Jacob

Viner, *Studies in the Theory of International Trade* (1937, reissued 1975); Michael D. Bordo and Anna Jacobson Schwartz (eds.), *A Retrospective on the Classical Gold Standard, 1821–1931* (1984); David E.W. Laidler, *The Demand for Money: Theories and Evidence*, 4th ed. (1993); Bennett T. McCallum, *Monetary Economics: Theory and Policy* (1989); and Irving Fisher, *The Purchasing Power of Money*, new ed. (1931, reissued 1997), a classic work on the velocity of money.

Capital Market Integration

Eric Helleiner, *States and the Reemergence of Global Finance* (1994); Anne-Marie Slaughter, *A New World Order* (2004).

On Marketing

The most widely used textbook is Philip Kotler, *Marketing Management: Analysis, Planning, Implementation, and Control*, 8th ed. (1994). Robert Bartels, *History of Marketing Thought*, 3rd ed. (1988), provides an overview of marketing through the years and contains an extensive bibliography. A more conceptual and theoretical treatment may be found in the work by Wroe Alderson, *Dynamic Marketing Behavior: A Functionalist Theory of Marketing* (1965).

Various strategic and tactical aspects of marketing are explored in the following studies: Steven P. Schnaars, *Marketing Strategy: A Customer-Driven Approach* (1991); Jack Trout and Al Reis, *Positioning: The Battle for Your Mind*, rev. ed. (1986); Thomas T. Nagle and Reed K. Holden, *The Strategy and Tactics of Pricing*, 2nd ed. (1994); Gilbert A. Churchill, Jr., Neil M. Ford, and Orville C. Walker, Jr., *Sales Force Management*, 4th ed. (1993); Don E. Schultz, Stanley I. Tannenbaum, and Robert F.

Lauterborn, *Integrated Marketing Communications* (1992); Mary Lou Roberts and Paul D. Berger, *Direct Marketing Management* (1989); David A. Aaker, *Strategic Market Management*, 3rd ed. (1991); Glen L. Urban and John Hauser, *Design and Marketing of New Products*, 2nd ed. (1993); and Stan Rapp and Thomas L. Collins, *Beyond Maximarketing* (1994). The importance of marketing intermediaries is outlined by Louis W. Stern and Adel I. El-Ansary, *Marketing Channels*, 4th ed. (1992).

Theodore Levitt, *The Marketing Imagination*, new, expanded ed. (1986); and Regis McKenna, *Relationship Marketing: Successful Strategies for the Age of the Customer* (1991), discuss the evolving discipline of marketing.

The role of marketing research is investigated in the extended work by Gilbert A. Churchill, Jr., *Marketing Research: Methodological Foundations*, 5th ed. (1991). The role the consumer plays in the marketing process is examined in Michael R. Solomon, *Consumer Behavior*, 2nd ed. (1994); and David A. Aaker and George S. Day, *Consumerism: Search for Consumer Interest*, 4th ed. (1982).

Advertising's role in the marketing process is explored in David Ogilvy, Ogilvy on Advertising (1983); John Lyons, *Guts: Advertising from the Inside Out* (1987); and William Wells, John Burnett, and Sandra Moriarty, *Advertising: Principles and Practice*, 2nd ed. (1992).

Marketing in several different sectors is dealt with in the following selected works: David A. Aaker and Alexander L. Biel, *Brand Equity & Advertising* (1993); David A. Aaker, *Managing Brand Equity* (1991); Christopher H. Lovelock, *Services Marketing*, 2nd ed. (1991), and *Managing Services: Marketing,*

Operations, and Human Resources, 2nd ed. (1991); Michael D. Hutt and Thomas W. Speh, *Business Marketing Management: A Strategic View of Industrial and Organizational Markets*, 4th ed. (1992); Philip Kotler and Alan R. Andreasen, *Strategic Marketing for Nonprofit Organizations*, 4th ed. (1991); Philip Kotler and Roberta N. Clarke, *Marketing for Healthcare Organizations* (1986); Philip Kotler and Eduardo Roberto, *Social Marketing: Strategies for Changing Public Behavior* (1989); Philip Kotler, Donald H. Heider, and Irving Rein, *Marketing Places: Attracting Investment, Industry, and Tourism to Cities, States, and Nations* (1993); and Michael R. Czinkota and Ilkka A. Ronkainen, *International Marketing*, 3rd ed. (1993).

Current marketing trends are reported in a number of trade journals and newspapers, including *Marketing News* (biweekly); *Marketing Management* (quarterly); *Journal of Retailing* (quarterly); *Advertising Age* (weekly); *Business Marketing* (monthly); *Harvard Business Review* (bimonthly); *Wall Street Journal* (daily); *Business Week* (weekly); *Fortune* (biweekly); *California Management Review* (quarterly); and *Business Horizons* (bimonthly). More scholarly research journals include *Journal of Marketing Research* (quarterly); *Journal of Marketing* (quarterly); *Journal of Consumer Research* (quarterly); and *Journal of the Academy of Marketing Science* (quarterly).

Consumption

The impetus for the modern consumption literature comes largely from John Maynard Keynes, *The General Theory of Employment, Interest, and Money* (1936); although Keynes's model of the consumption function has been superseded, there is still much wisdom in his discussion. The two classic references that form the foundation of the modern life-cycle and permanent-income theories of consumption are Franco

Modigliani and Richard Brumberg, "Utility Analysis and the Consumption Function: An Interpretation of Cross-Section Data," in Kenneth K. Kurihara (ed.), *Post-Keynesian Economics* (1954, reissued 1993), pp. 388–436; and Milton Friedman, *A Theory of the Consumption Function* (1957). An excellent summary of the literature can be found in Angus Deaton, Understanding Consumption (1992). An overview of the current baseline model and of the relationship between the mathematically rigorous versions of the life-cycle and permanent-income-hypothesis models is given in Christopher D. Carroll (1997), "Buffer-Stock Saving and the Life Cycle/Permanent Income Hypothesis," *The Quarterly Journal of Economics*, 107(1):1–56 (1997).

Perspectives that deviate from the current baseline framework have a venerable history, starting with Adam Smith, *An Inquiry into the Nature and Causes of the Wealth of Nations* (1776); of particular interest is chapter 2, where Smith argues that people care about how their consumption compares to that of others. Thorstein Veblen, *The Theory of the Leisure Class* (1899, reissued 1998), provides an extended treatment of this idea and introduces the phrase "conspicuous consumption." Many related issues are discussed in Robert H. Frank, *Choosing the Right Pond* (1985). The introduction of Christopher D. Carroll, Jody Overland, and David N. Weil, "Saving and Growth with Habit Formation," *American Economic Review*, 90(3):341–355 (2000), gives a summary of the evidence that habit formation may play an important role in explaining a wide variety of puzzles in macroeconomics. The seminal paper in the modern literature on self-control problems in consumption is David Laibson, "Golden Eggs and Hyperbolic Discounting," *The Quarterly Journal of Economics*, 112(2):443–477 (1997).

The Business Cycle

The impetus for the modern consumption literature comes largely from John Maynard Keynes, *The General Theory of Employment, Interest, and Money* (1936); although Keynes's model of the consumption function has been superseded, there is still much wisdom in his discussion. The two classic references that form the foundation of the modern life-cycle and permanent-income theories of consumption are Franco Modigliani and Richard Brumberg, "Utility Analysis and the Consumption Function: An Interpretation of Cross-Section Data," in Kenneth K. Kurihara (ed.), *Post-Keynesian Economics* (1954, reissued 1993), pp. 388–436; and Milton Friedman, *A Theory of the Consumption Function* (1957). An excellent summary of the literature can be found in Angus Deaton, Understanding Consumption (1992). An overview of the current baseline model and of the relationship between the mathematically rigorous versions of the life-cycle and permanent-income-hypothesis models is given in Christopher D. Carroll (1997), "Buffer-Stock Saving and the Life Cycle/Permanent Income Hypothesis," *The Quarterly Journal of Economics*, 107(1):1–56 (1997).

Perspectives that deviate from the current baseline framework have a venerable history, starting with Adam Smith, *An Inquiry into the Nature and Causes of the Wealth of Nations* (1776); of particular interest is chapter 2, where Smith argues that people care about how their consumption compares to that of others. Thorstein Veblen, *The Theory of the Leisure Class* (1899, reissued 1998), provides an extended treatment of this idea and introduces the phrase "conspicuous consumption." Many related issues are discussed in Robert H. Frank, *Choosing the Right Pond* (1985). The introduction of Christopher D. Carroll, Jody Overland, and David N. Weil, "Saving and

Growth with Habit Formation," *American Economic Review*, 90(3):341–355 (2000), gives a summary of the evidence that habit formation may play an important role in explaining a wide variety of puzzles in macroeconomics. The seminal paper in the modern literature on self-control problems in consumption is David Laibson, "Golden Eggs and Hyperbolic Discounting," *The Quarterly Journal of Economics*, 112(2):443–477 (1997).

Market Busts

Stuart W. Leslie, *The Cold War and American Science: The Military-Industrial-Academic Complex at MIT and Stanford* (1993), is a critical history of the growth of government-funded academic research, including early programs at MIT and Stanford from World War II. AnnaLee Saxenian, *Regional Advantage: Culture and Competition in Silicon Valley and Route 128* (1994), compares and contrasts the growth of high-technology companies around Stanford and MIT. C. Stewart Gillmor, *Fred Terman at Stanford: Building a Discipline, a University, and Silicon Valley* (2004), is a fine biography of Silicon Valley's founder.

Economics

Mark Blaug and Howard R. Vane (eds.), *Who's Who in Economics*, 4th ed. (2003), contains biographical information on 1,500 economists, based on their frequency of citation in economics journals. Mark Blaug, *Great Economists Before Keynes* (1986, reissued 1997), provides thumbnail sketches of the ideas of 200 eminent economists. Douglas Greenwald (ed.), *The McGraw-Hill Encyclopaedia of Economics*, 2nd ed. (1994); and Phillip Anthony O'Hara (ed.), *Encyclopaedia of Political Economy*,

2 vol. (1998, reissued 2001), are two accessible sources of reference addressed to students coming to economics for the first time.

There is the more comprehensive John Eatwell, Murray Milgate, and Peter Newman (eds.), *The New Palgrave: A Dictionary of Economics*, 4 vol. (1987, reissued 2002), but the level of readability and technical difficulty varies greatly from entry to entry. For a more accessible overview, see Roger E. Backhouse, *The Penguin History of Economics* (2002).

Representative introductory textbooks are Paul A. Samuelson and William D. Nordhaus, *Economics*, 18th ed. (2005); Richard G. Lipsey and K. Alec Chrystal, *Economics*, 10th ed. (2004); and William J. Baumol and Alan S. Blinder, Economics: *Principles and Policy*, 9th ed. (2003).

Economic Growth

Simon Kuznets, *Capital in the American Economy: Its Formation and Financing* (1961), a description of trends in capital formation in different sectors of the American economy from the mid-19th to the mid-20th century; W.W. Rostow, *The Stages of Economic Growth*, 2nd ed. (1971); Ezra J. Mishan, *The Cost of Economic Growth* (1967), a critique of rapid economic growth as a policy goal; John Kenneth Galbraith, *The Affluent Society*, 4th ed. (1984), a critique of modern capitalism written for the layman; Joseph A. Schumpeter, *Business Cycles: A Theoretical, Historical, and Statistical Analysis of the Capitalist Process*, 2 vol. (1939, reprinted 1982), a pioneering work in the field of growth and cycles that stresses the importance of entrepreneurship; and James S. Duesenberry, *Business Cycles and Economic Growth* (1958, reprinted 1977), a theoretical study of a developed economy of the American type, with emphasis on the importance of demand in growth. Later studies include Dan Usher, *The Measurement of Economic Growth* (1980), an explanation of the difficulties inherent in such measurement; John Cornwall, *The Conditions for Economic Recovery: A Post-Keynesian Analysis* (1983), an analysis of the causes and consequences of economic stagnation; Martin Ricketts, *The New Industrial Economics: An Introduction to Modern Theories of the Firm* (1987), stressing the role of entrepreneurship in modern economics; and on government intervention, Stephen Wilks and Maurice Wright (eds.), *Comparative Government-Industry Relations: Western Europe, the United States, and Japan* (1987).

Productivity

General works dealing with productivity and its measurement include John W. Kendrick, *Understanding Productivity* (1977); John W. Kendrick and Elliot S. Grossman, *Productivity in the United States* (1980); Jean Fourastié, *La Productivité*, 10th ed. (1980); and Gerhart E. Reuss, *Produktivitätsanalyse: Ökonomische Grundlagen und statistische Methodik* (1960). See also United States. Bureau of Labor Statistics, Productivity: A Selected Annotated Bibliography (irregular); and *Trends in Multifactor Productivity, 1948–81* (1983), updated annually by the news release *Multifactor Productivity Measures*. Estimates of the growth of output, inputs, and productivity are presented in the *OECD Economic Outlook* (semiannual), providing coverage for major countries of the world. In Edward F. Denison, *Trends in American Economic Growth, 1929–1982* (1985), the author uses the "growth accounting" method that he pioneered. An early work on international comparisons of output and productivity is Colin Clark, *The Conditions of Economic Progress*, 3rd ed. (1957, reprinted 1983). Later works include Edward F. Denison, *Why Growth Rates Differ: Postwar Experience in Nine Western Countries* (1967)—updated by John W. Kendrick, "International Comparison of Recent Productivity Trends," in William Fellner (ed.), *Essays in Contemporary Economic Problems* (1981); Angus Maddison, "Growth and Slowdown in Advanced Capitalist Economies: Techniques of Quantitative Assessment," *Journal of Economic Literature*, 25(2):649–98 (June 1987), and the same author's *Phases of Capitalist Development* (1982). World-wide comparisons are made in Irving A. Kravis and Robert E. Lipsey, "The Diffusion of Economic Growth in the World Economy, 1950–80," in John W. Kendrick (ed.), *International Comparisons of Productivity and Causes of the Slowdown* (1984). The convergence thesis is examined in William J. Baumol, "Productivity Growth, Convergence, and Welfare: What the Long-Run Data Show," *The American Economic Review*, 76(5):1072–85 (December 1986).

INDEX